THE SCARLET THREAD

THE SCARLET THREAD
An Indian Woman Speaks

Her story as told to Rachel Barton

With an Afterword by
Yasmin Alibhai & Pragna Patel

Published by VIRAGO PRESS Limited 1987
41 William IV Street, London WC2N 4DB

Copyright © Rachel Barton 1987

British Library Cataloguing in Publication Data

Barton, Rachel
  The scarlet thread: an Indian woman speaks.
  1. Arranged marriage—Great Britain
  2. Women, East Indian—Great Britain
  I. Title
  306.8'4   HQ614

ISBN 0-86068-871-2

Typeset by Florencetype Ltd, Kewstoke, Avon
Printed in Great Britain by
Cox and Wyman Ltd, Reading, Berkshire

The photograph on the front cover is of a model,
not of the central character in the book.

To our two mothers, one Indian, one British,
both alike in courage

Introduction

There are many Asians living in my part of the city and I used to watch the women in the streets and in the shops and wonder about them. They looked strange in their bright exotic dress in this grey place. Though I would have liked to have known about them I knew they were deep in their world and I in mine and I never expected the two worlds to meet. That was before I came to know Sita.*

It happened by chance through the voluntary work I was doing, for there I met Sister Magdalene, a nun well known in our locality for her tireless and loving efforts to help those most in need. She asked me if I would give lessons in English to Sita, and befriend her and her family. I said I would be glad to, and soon she came to see me. I had noticed that Asian women often looked sad but few looked as sad as Sita. My heart went out to her and we soon became friends.

To encourage her to speak more fluently I asked her to tell me about her childhood in India. From this in the course of a year or more she gradually revealed the story of her brief life. I was deeply moved by her experiences and the way she expressed her thoughts and feelings, and started to write down what she told me. Through her touching and tragic story I entered to some extent that world which I thought closed to me. Eventually with Sita's agreement I pieced together the events of her life to make this book. It is true to her own viewpoint and I have tried as far as possible to keep it in her own words.

Rachel Barton, July 1986

---

* The name Sita is a pseudonym.

My name is Sita Devi. I was born in a small village in north-west India twenty-eight years ago. Now I am a British citizen and I have lived in the UK for nearly thirteen years. I know something of how people here live; I have visited their homes, seen their family life, heard about their work and joined them in their leisure; I even know something about the way they think. But the people here know nothing of how we live at home in India, or even how we live over here so close to them.

Sometimes they think they know better than I do. A school teacher I spoke to once said, 'It must be terrible for you in India to see so many people ill and starving around you.' I said, 'But I have not seen this; everyone in our village had enough to eat, even the poorest, and most were quite healthy.' He became angry and started to shout at me. 'You are so ignorant, you must know that Indian people are starving.'

I can only tell of what I have seen, or know for certain, and I will write everything as truly as I can. I do not think that any Indian woman has done this before, certainly not an uneducated girl like me. Perhaps there are some things I have not understood correctly, or have not paid enough attention to. It is only in the last year or so that I have started to think about my life. Now my English friend is writing down for me what I tell her.

Most people here seem to think we live in shacks in India, all crowded together, with everything dirty and wretched about us. It may be so for some in the big cities, but I will tell you how we lived in our village of about one thousand people.

All around us are the plains, stretching far far away, where many crops are grown — wheat and maize, sugar cane, vegetables, and the yellow-flowered mustard. Roses grow on the hedges between the fields. Our village is beautiful, quite like an English village. There are many trees in the squares and beside the houses. Many people have a little land and grow flowers and vegetables. The trees give welcome shade and are useful for tethering animals. Our tree is very tall and very old, it is called a 'Nime'. There are many canals in our part of the country, some of them like big rivers with smaller branches bringing water to every part of the land. One such canal flows near our village. The water is clean and clear and we can see little fishes in it. There is also a lake, and here the farmers take their buffaloes and oxen and other animals to drink. Roads leading to and from the village are lined with fine shady trees, some of which have flowers and fruit in season, like the chatoot and behr, and we can pick them as we go along. As children we loved to do this.

The village streets are rather narrow, but this makes them shady in hot weather. Some houses, their outer walls smooth and red, are made of clay which we fetch from the edge of the lake. Others are more modern and made of cement, brick or concrete. Our house is partly clay and part brick. It belongs to my father, who had it from his father. Now my second brother lives there with his family. The roof is flat and we can sit there in the day and sleep there in the hot season as most people do. It is lovely to lie under the still sky and watch the moon and the stars, very big and bright. We have very light beds made of a wooden frame covered with woven material, and these can be easily taken up to the roof and down again. This is useful if it suddenly starts to rain in the night and we have to hurry to shelter. If it turns cold we do not worry as we have quilts to cover us. The women and children sleep in one part and the men in another, or on the verandahs. The older women would often tell stories to us children, or read from a book. We had electricity in our house, and could bring a wire up from downstairs if we wished. Other times we would all sing together.

There is a courtyard in front of our house and a big room on the ground floor. We did not live in this room but every day one of my elder sisters would wash it over in preparation for the neighbours to come. Five or six women from our street would come every forenoon to sit with us, bringing their food and their work. We all sat on woven rugs on the floor. They made baskets and mats and bedcovers, did embroidery or made up saris. Others would bring baskets of grain and pick out the stones and grit before it was ground. These things they made were for their homes or, if unmarried, for their dowries. There would be much gossiping, laughing, singing, or sometimes quarrelling. I sat and listened to them, but as the youngest I did not work. I enjoyed the company and all the interest of their talk, and learned much about the village. It was impossible to be bored or lonely in our house. When the time for the evening meal drew near all the women went away to prepare for the men coming home from work.

Behind the big room there are two smaller rooms. One of these is used by the women as a bathroom and is also a grain store. My mother had made this store herself out of cement, and it is like a big deep box, always filled with wheat or maize. She did not buy the grain but earned it by her work as a seamstress. We had so much we could always sell some of it. In this room were two big iron buckets that were filled with water from a hand pump just outside. This was spring water, also used for cooking. Every day we poured the water from the buckets over ourselves or, when we were young, our mother would do it for us. This is the normal custom in the village. Mother used to get up at four o'clock in the morning, and even if it was cold, pour water over herself from the pump to wake herself up; she had to work so hard. Then she would often make our dinner before she went to work. The men washed in a little shed beside the house near the hand pump. On our small piece of land we also had a garden where Mother grew vegetables and flowers, and there was a shed for the animals. Most villagers keep a cow and a buffalo if they can afford it. Buffalo milk is very rich. We made our own butter, using a small hand churn, and had the butter-milk to drink. We also made our own cheese, but we did not have a buffalo after we became poorer. Some people keep goats too. All these animals are sometimes kept in the ground-floor room, but we never did this.

Every day my brother would go on his bike to the farmer to buy grass for the animals, bringing it back in a big cloth, as we had no grazing. This was not enough for them so we gave them household scraps and fodder bought from the store. Every day, too, they must be taken to the canal to drink and refresh themselves. Otherwise they were just tethered. One bad thing about the village was the flies, and that was the same, I think, everywhere in India. Having the animals so near attracts them, and although we had sprays to kill them they always seemed just as numerous. Mosquitoes too are horrible, especially in those days when few families had nets, and at night our happy sleep was often disturbed by them.

Upstairs was our living room and bedrooms. Although we usually sit on the floor on mats, we had chairs here, and a settee made by hand out of wood. There was also a big wooden bed where sometimes my father or brother slept. Married people do not sleep in the same bed, or even in the same room, unless they are newly weds. This is very different from the custom over here. In fact, we all sleep in various places as we can so easily put our mats and quilts down on the floor, which is always kept very clean. There were nine people in my family so we had several cupboards for our clothes, and ropes slung across the corners where more things could be hung. Our meals were often cooked outside in the courtyard in an earthenware stove that could be carried about. It was filled with wood or coal or dried cow dung, which we would light and wait until it was really hot, then we could cook on top. It may seem odd to use cow dung, but it is good fuel. It is made into round 'cakes' when still wet, and then thrown against the side of the house to dry. We had several other stoves — one was for paraffin — so we could cook many dishes at once.

While in Britain people tend to live behind closed doors; ours in the village are always open. It is never really cold, even in winter, and we can live very much outside. We also like to do things together and we do not lead private lives in the village. For instance, morning and evening when we used to go to the toilet, the women would go in one direction and the men in another, just to the fields. We would squat down among the grass and bushes and make it quite a social occasion. Hindus are bodily very clean; we wash all over each day and wash our hands before meals. We must wash our private parts after going to the toilet, so we usually take water with us. Some villagers had cesspits near their houses, a few had flush toilets, but they did not always use them. One year a village man who had worked in England wrote and told his family that he was returning with his bride, a wealthy English girl. The parents improved their house and even bought and installed a flush toilet for her use. She was very friendly and stayed a long time, but when she left the toilet was not used as it was too good to use.

2

I have never been able to return to my village so I do not know how it is now, but many Indians do go home and they tell me about the changes there. It is remarkable, but there is hardly a family without some member in the UK. Most of them work hard and make money, and much of it is sent back home to their own families. Because of this, and because there is now gas and electricity for all, there is more convenience than before. Many have built fine new houses, just as good as the ones we see in the suburbs over here, and inside there are TV sets, gas stoves, washing machines and refrigerators, as well as modern furniture and ornaments. I have noticed that there are good things and bad things in my part of India, and different good things and bad things here. This is rather confusing. When some things that are good here are taken to the Indian village, like washing machines, it improves life in some ways but spoils it in others. For instance, when I was a child the women would carry their big wash to the lake together, taking the children and food for a picnic. Sitting at the edge of the water with their soap and washboards they would rub the clothes clean as they talked and sang and argued as usual. The children would run around and play together, and when it was time to eat, fires would be lit, tea made, and chapatis cooked with other delicious things to eat. No one was in a hurry and the summer days were long. All these things the women did together made them close, and usually they would help each other in time of need.

There were grocery shops in the village, but no others. To buy other things we had to go to the nearest town or wait for a fair to pass by. Since shop goods were dear and not as well made as those made at home, most village people seldom bought them. So the women and girls were always busy making things in ways they had learned from their mothers and grandmothers. My sisters were also very clever in this way and could make quilts and pillowcases, saris and blouses, and decorate them with embroidery. These things were often beautiful, and very skilfully made; the women enjoyed making them and were proud of their good work. Now people in the village have more money and travel more to the towns. They can get cheap goods there and it does not seem worthwhile to make their own.

Oxen were always used to draw the plough, pull carts and so on, but now I hear that tractors and other kinds of machinery are used by many farmers. This is another reason why the village is better off. Perhaps the farm animals will go in time, but I hope I will be able to go back home before everything is changed too much. Some improvements I will enjoy if I do go; for instance, a new ice factory and the many new shops in the village.

Most Indian women love dress; it is a very important part of our lives. I have always done so, even as a small girl. Because my mother worked as a seamstress she had many pieces of material kept in a big chest. I loved to see all the different colours and feel the textures of the cloth, and I was always begging for new dresses or tunics and trousers. Little girls in the village could wear bright and pretty clothes until they started their periods. After that they should dress very quietly and wear their hair simply braided in one plait. Girls looked forward to marriage because then they could wear beautiful saris, denied to unmarried girls, use make-up, and wear jewellery of gold and silver. Although we were quite poor I always had lovely clothes because of my mother, but I never felt I had enough. I wanted to dress like the wealthier girls in the village, so sometimes I would steal some pretty pieces from my mother's chest and persuade a neighbour to make me a dress. Then mother would be angry because she was keeping the materials for our dowries.

When I was about five years old I longed to wear earrings,

so I took a long sharp thorn and pushed the point into my ear lobe. It hurt me and the end broke off and stayed in my ear. I never told anyone and it is still there! Soon after I heard that a neighbour was piercing ears with a needle and thread, so I went along and asked her to do mine. Two friends held me still while she pushed the needle through, but it was very painful and I screamed and struggled as she did the other ear. Afterwards I was glad. She left a piece of thread in each hole to keep it open, but now I know that she should have sterilised the needle, as my ears became infected and for some time I had sores on both sides. It was about three months before they cleared up, and when I put my earrings in the infection started again because they were made of cheap metal, not silver, gold or steel. That did not stop me loving to wear earrings, as I still do.

One day my vanity led me into more trouble. Like most Indian girls I had long thick black hair which I wore in a plait. It was the fashion for little girls at that time to wear ribbon bows in white or bright colours in their hair. Some of the better-off children had two plaits and two bows, so I did the same. My eldest brother Krishna was much older than me, and was studying at the university. Because Mother and Father were away a great deal he was head of the house, and with six younger children, five girls and one boy, this was a big responsibility. He took it very seriously and was so strict with us that we feared and disliked him. He often hit us very hard if we annoyed him; if the pots and pans were not clean enough, for instance, or if we were untidy. When he came home that day and saw my plaits he fell into a rage. He seized me, and taking a pair of scissors cut off one plait and threw it over the verandah. Crying from shock and distress I ran down to the courtyard and picked up my lovely long plait, still with its ribbon. Now I looked terrible with half my hair cut off close to the scalp.

When Mother came home I ran to show her what he had done and she was angry with Krishna and shouted at him. But he was grown-up and educated and much the cleverest in the family, so he always got the better of her and everyone else. My auntie who was with us at the time said, 'Don't worry, all the girls in Delhi are cutting their hair short now, and I will cut the rest of yours.' But of course it looked dreadful and I had to wear a veil over my head until it grew. Luckily it grew even longer and glossier than before. When he left home and used to visit us, my brother was quite different, kind and gentle even, but it took us some time to trust him. I understand now why he was so strict. Indian parents and older sisters and brothers are very much afraid of their young girls becoming interested in sex and attracting boys, as they may become pregnant before marriage. They think they must stop even innocent little girls of five or seven looking too attractive in case it gives them ideas.

3

It is time I told you about my family. My father and mother were both of the tailoring caste. This is a middling sort of caste with some above us and some below. As you probably know we usually have to marry within the caste, and this is true even in Britain. I believe this custom is dying out amongst some educated people. My parents had ten children, but three died young. The ones who lived were my eldest brother Krishna, my second brother Veejay, and the girls, Sheelah the eldest, then Indira, Prem and Asha in order, with me Sita the youngest girl. When they were first married, my parents were quite well off, but by the time I was born they were poor; I will explain why later. So my mother had to work as well as my father, but because she had been respected in the village she never worked there but preferred to go every day to surrounding villages, sometimes as far as six or seven miles away. Every day she would walk there and back with her sewing machine on her shoulder, unless there was a wedding or other special occasion when she would stay the night. It would have been dangerous for her to walk back alone in the dark as there were sometimes bad men about who might have attacked her. She was popular with the farmers and their wives for whom she worked, so at these feasts they would give her plenty of food to take home, enough for several days.

I have never heard of any other mother who did so much for her family and loved them all so well. When she was not sewing for other families she would sew for us, making clothes and everything we needed in the house. I never saw her idle, for she would cook and clean and milk the animals and look after the garden. I always wanted to be near her and would sleep near her wherever she was. While she was away I longed for her, sometimes so much that when my sisters or brothers were angry with me I would run out of the house and look for her in the villages, sometimes running for miles. Mother meant everything to us and she took responsibility for everything. As she could not be with us very much she was very firm, even stern, and we were frightened to offend her. We did not resent this for we knew she loved us and wanted our good.

I often wondered how Mother could live with so little sleep. She only lay down on her bed when she was ill, and this did not often happen. Then she would refuse to see a doctor or take any medicine; in spite of this she always recovered quite soon. In the evening when others were resting after a day's work she would sit cross-legged on the floor on her blanket in front of her sewing machine, the light bulb pulled down low over her head so that she could see to work. During the night she would doze off from time to time and her head would drop forward, but she would wake with a jerk and go on sewing. Less often she would sink down onto her blanket and sleep a little. I know just how it was because as usual I slept close to her.

Often there were three or four girls from our street — one rich girl, a friend of Asha's, my next elder sister, and sometimes more girls from around — who would come to spend the evening and perhaps bring their quilts and stay the night. It was Mother who attracted them because she was lively and friendly and stayed up so late while their mothers went early to bed. The girls would bring their books to study when exams were near. Mother would say to them, 'Read aloud to me, then I will know you are really studying.' She would listen as she sewed and one girl after another read from her book.

Sometimes about midnight we would make tea to refresh ourselves. It was like having a night party and I loved it. If we had no tea or milk I would go with the girls to a neighbour's house and knock on the door to wake them up and shout, 'Open up the shop, we need tea and milk.' Sometimes they would curse and grumble, but we would say, 'Please help us, we have exams tomorrow.' This would make them sorry for us, so someone would take a lantern and go to the shop to sell us the tea and milk. If no one would help us we would do without and boil up some fennel leaves instead. How often later I was to remember those happy times and wonder if girls in the village were still the same.

In the morning Mother would call us early and take each girl to the pump and wake her up properly with the cold water. If there were exams that day we were always given fresh yoghurt just before we left to clear our brains. Mother knew how important it was for us to have a good education and pass our exams. She was sorry she had not had our chances, but in spite of this she was very clever in many ways. She had never learned tailoring but had taught herself to make beautiful clothes; with her machine she did embroidery, inventing all the designs herself, each one different. Watching her I learned to make doll's clothes, and these were so pretty that other girls wanted them too. I had an idea; I went round the village shops and sold them to the girls who worked there. Unfortunately the girls were so tempted by my doll's clothes that they took money from the till to buy them. When Mother heard of this it was the end of my little business. She would not tolerate dishonesty of any kind.

My father was a trained tailor and he too worked outside the village, going further afield and staying away for days or even weeks. He would stop in a farmhouse to make clothes and also to teach the women how to use the sewing machine. There he would have his food and not work too hard, but he did not earn much. When he returned home he would often bring nothing but sweets and cakes for the children. Then my poor mother would be very angry. 'Don't take the sweets', she would say, 'they are not good for you, and will only make him think he has done something when he has done nothing.' We could not respect Father much when he left all the burdens to Mother. He did have some excuse for being this way because he had a cousin who had gone to live in Canada and had done very well in business. He had promised my father that he would send for him and employ him so that he

too would become wealthy. Waiting for this to happen unsettled my father, but his cousin kept putting it off until
eventually he died.

Father would have been a wealthy man himself if he had
been more lucky. His father had a good business, a big shop
in the town selling groceries of all kinds. His first two sons
were much older than Father and they worked in the business with him. The younger brother Ramesh married his
cousin Sonia, and she took over the care of my father, bringing him up as her own child. My two uncles were always
taking goods and money from the shop for themselves, and
this meant the business declined. Uncle Ramesh took enough
to educate his sons and marry off his daughters. Very little of
it was spent on Father. Aunty Sonia saved up what she could
until she had a treasure in gold and silver.

When Grandfather died the shop and the three houses
were left, as is the custom, to his sons. Father got one of the
houses, the one in which we lived and which is still in the
family. Father should have had his share of the shop, too, but
my uncles secretly took all the stock of non-perishable items
and hid them. Then they closed the shop. Soon after they
opened a new shop with all the stock they had taken. My
father was still too young to know that they had cheated him
and he never had his share. His two brothers prospered
while he remained poor.

When Father married my mother, Uncle Ramesh and
Aunty Sonia lived nearby. I remember them well. Aunty was
old and blind by that time, and as a little girl I was very fond
of her. I used to lead her out into the fields to enjoy the open
air. She would ask me to pick mustard leaves for her; she
would taste each one and tell me which were the best ones to
choose. Then she would take a bunch back to her daughter-
in-law for her to use in curries.

Aunty knew that when we five daughters were born it was
a great worry for our parents and she used to say, 'Cheer up,
I will help you. I have money hidden for you.' Mother always
hoped she would tell her where it was before she died. She
used to look after Aunty very kindly, not only for the money
but because she was naturally kind to everyone. They were

well off from having the shop and another house in the village, and they lived well. It was hard for us sometimes, for when we had little to eat in the house we could walk past their place and smell the good food they were cooking. All we ever had from Aunty was buttermilk. Each day she would bring a big bowl of it to the gate and call out. Buttermilk is good, but it is so plentiful that the village people even throw it away or wash their hair with it.

When Aunty died I was far away but Mother told me that the treasure remained hidden. Perhaps her daughter-in-law found it. I sometimes wonder if it is still there somewhere, or did she just pretend that she had it? We will never know.

The burdens on our family were very great with seven children to educate and see into marriage. Schooling in India is free only to the very poorest, and though it costs little at the village school it is more at the big high school in the town. All books must be paid for, and the uniform too. My eldest brother who was so clever won scholarships, but he had to be fed and clothed and given pocket money when other young men were earning. Nearly all this came from Mother's work, and what she could not earn she had to borrow, either from relatives or the village moneylender. To pay for five girls to be married is an appalling burden, for without a good dowry there is little chance of a good husband. All marriages in the village were arranged, and much bargaining took place. If there is no money to go with the bride she must bring many fine saris, gold and jewellery, bed quilts and mats, and these days perhaps TV sets, washing machines and other expensive goods. The bridegroom must be given fine clothes at least. Most of all, the wedding feast costs thousands of rupees. My mother worried and worried about these things, which had to be done or else the whole family would be utterly disgraced. This is one reason why girl babies are not welcomed in the family. When a boy is born there is rejoicing. A party is given, sweets presented to all, and there is song and dance. This is not done when a girl is born.

Even boys cost their parents some money, but nothing like as much. The bride must be given rich presents, and more exchanged between the in-laws. Then for the first year at least the bride goes to live with her husband's family. Once a girl is married, even if her husband becomes very rich and her own family is poor, they should expect nothing from her. When they go to visit her they must take gifts but accept nothing in return. They do not even eat food or drink water in her house. A man who marries can be expected to help his own family if he can afford it, but many do not do so. Krishna, who had so much help in his life from his mother, never did, and she would never ask or reproach him.

Mother had to arrange Krishna's marriage, and this is what happened. He was by then over thirty and was in a good job as a college lecturer, but he had refused to marry before some of his sisters at least had been found husbands. In spite of his education he did not wish to break away from our tradition and was happy to accept an arranged marriage. When he was asked if he would like to see his bride before he married her in case she was not pretty, he said, 'Not all girls can be beautiful. I have five sisters who need husbands. What if they should be rejected because they are not good-looking enough?' Mother used to ask everyone in the village if they knew of a suitable bride for him. At length she was told of a family in Delhi who had a marriageable daughter. So far all her efforts and enquiries had come to nothing, so although this family was rather poor and not specially suitable, she arranged to meet them. Krishna should have had a good choice, as he was not only well qualified but good-looking as well, but he was in a hurry after waiting so long and being on his own in a strange place. So Mother took her sister and my sister Indira and went to Delhi to arrange matters.

To their surprise, the other side insisted that they met in the temple so that anything said should be binding in such a holy place. They were disappointed in the girl, who was plain and had a big mole on her neck, which is unlucky as well as ugly, but her mother and aunts talked them into accepting. If they had had time to think it over I believe they would have changed their minds, but they were told that they must decide right away or the whole thing would be called off. They also had to pay a marriage fee then and there, and being in the temple made it harder to refuse, as the other side well knew. Only then were Mother and her party invited to tea in their house. When we told Krishna he was not too pleased, but he had to put up with it. Indians do not expect to be in love when they marry, for marriage is a sort of business arrangement, and if there is attraction, or if love grows, that is a bonus. Sadesh and he were married, and he brought her home, but although we tried to be friendly and kind she did not seem to like us and would not stay, although this is the custom. She had two daughters but they both died at birth and she can have no more. Now they live in Delhi and are well off, but not, I have heard, happy. Sadesh will not let Krishna send money to his family, nor will she let him marry again to have children. If she gave her consent he could do this, as many do in India. It is done here too, but I do not know if it is legal. I think it is done on the quiet.

Mother wanted us all to have a good education, even the girls, because although we would certainly be getting married and perhaps never work outside the home, a girl with education is worth more in marriage. This is very important if there is no dowry. Of course, times are changing and it is becoming more usual for women who have had training to work outside the home. My eldest sister Sheelah trained as a teacher; she too was quite clever. Indira learned handicrafts in college; Prem took nurse's training and she too did well; Asha studied to be a secretary. Mother was proud to have educated daughters. She herself had had little opportunity, but she was unusually independent and strong-minded.

There was one special sorrow in our family; the second son Veejay had a terrible accident. It came about this way. Far away in the mountains to the north is the famous shrine of the Maharanee Shiva chert purnee, a goddess with eight arms who sits on a lion. She appeared to some children there long ago as the Virgin Mary appeared to Bernadette in Lourdes. She asked that a shrine be built there in her honour, and there is now a great temple. Many Hindus and others make pilgrimage to pray to her and may stay away for months. My parents went and took my brother Veejay. One day he was riding his bicycle down a steep mountain road when the brakes failed and he ran into a lorry. His back was badly injured and he was in hospital for several years, off and on. He never recovered completely. Like schools, hospitals in India are not free, so Mother had to find the money for treatment and medicines. It made us all very sad to see him an invalid, his career ruined. Even now, when my brother is living in our family house with his wife and children, he is not yet cured. He does odd jobs in the village but he is not well off. Mother never retired; she went on working to repay the debts she had incurred for us children. By the time she died, every one had been paid up, but the sad thing was that she did not live long enough to enjoy her freedom.

4

A lecturer at the university here, an Indian man, was talking to an English girlfriend of mine. He was complaining about the class system in this country. She asked him, 'Surely the caste system in India is much worse?' He replied, 'Oh the caste system in India has practically disappeared.' This is not what I have found in my life, and in fact the caste system is brought over here to Britain and is just as strong, at least among the people I know.

At home in the village the Untouchables live just outside in their own hamlet. Most of the villagers are fairly well off, but these people are poor and are allowed to do only the most menial work. The men are often field labourers; they may handle the grain but must not touch the flour as it would become contaminated. So it is not only that they must not touch people of higher caste, they must not touch their food or their possessions. The women have the worst jobs of all; they clean out the cesspits and stables and wash the streets. They are not usually paid in money, but in food, often that which is left over, and old clothing. They may never enter our houses, so they must bring their own dishes and we hand them the food outside.

It may seem strange that such customs are accepted as being quite natural, and I have never been told why it is, or how it started. At the same time, we can be friendly with the Harijan, as they prefer to be called, and help them when they are in trouble as long as they keep their distance. In fact in our family we do not really believe in caste as we belong to a special sect and have a famous guru, the Baba Charon Singh Maharaj. He is the third guru; my grandparents joined his sect, so we belong to it too. Because of his teachings we are strict vegetarians, refusing not only meat and fish but also eggs, unlike most Hindus who will eat meat other than beef (the cow is a sacred animal), fish and eggs.

When I went to school I became friendly with a Harijan girl called Vilma. She was in my class, but like all the Harijans she had to sit apart from us, for even as children we are told not to let them touch us. I was never able to visit her nor could she come to our house, in spite of the fact that our guru teaches us that all people are equal in the sight of God. We have to fit in with what our neighbours believe. The feeling about caste is very strong and difficult to overcome, even amongst the followers of our guru. I knew this from what my mother did one day. I was walking home from school with Vilma and she took my arm. I was quite happy about this, but my mother saw us and was very upset. As soon as I got in she made me take off my clothes and wash all over. Then she washed my clothes! She knew it was wrong, and she was a very religious woman, devoted to the guru, but she could not stop herself. Somehow or other I never felt like this about Untouchables or the castes above or below me.

In spite of their poverty and the way they are treated, some Untouchables do well in life. If they are clever they get scholarships and go to college; some rise high in government or go into business and become very rich. But this does not change their caste; they remain Untouchable even if they are millionaires! Over here they are known to other Hindus, who will not visit them or have them as guests in their homes, and of course to marry into their caste would be unthinkable. Everyone in the Hindu community knows this but it is not talked about. My friend Vilma married and came to live here in Leicester. Her husband is very hard-working and has done well; he sends money home to his family so his old mother and father do not have to work, and he has helped his brothers and sisters to get education and marry. Here he has a good house with modern furniture, a TV and video, and every comfort. They can afford to go back to India on visits with their three children. I am able to be close to my friend and we visit each other freely. She has helped me in hard times and lent me money, and in a way our positions are reversed, for in this country she is now the superior one while I am poor and not respected. British people of course do not know or care about caste, which is good for the Harijan, but Vilma and her husband do not have any white friends. It will be better for their children to be brought up here as equals in society.

I have said that ours is a middling caste, for not counting the Harijans who, strictly speaking, are outside the caste system, there is one below us. They can come into our houses and often do work for us. We would not do housework for others, but here in Leicester I am not ashamed to do housework for one of my friends and earn a little extra money. I no longer believe it matters, but my family still do and are shocked and think I am lowering myself. As well as tailors, like my parents, our caste tends to do skilled work or be tradesmen or farmers. The highest caste of course is the Brahmins. People here seem to think they are all superior, but just as the Harijans can be rich and successful, so the Brahmins can be poor and unsuccessful. Many of them become doctors, lawyers, teachers or priests, and in fact all Brahmins are automatically priests as theirs is the priestly caste. There were many Brahmins in our village, but not all of them are highly thought of. Some cast horoscopes and tell fortunes, and may make a living this way like gypsies. Brahmin priests perform all the temple rites and pray at weddings, funerals and so on. Their prayers are all in Sanscrit, so most people do not understand them.

The government would like us to do away with caste so that everyone would be equal, able to mix together and marry anyone they pleased. They have also tried to help the poor farmers and those without any land by passing a law to stop any one family owning too much land, but no one seems to take much notice. The custom of giving dowries and spending so much money on weddings is also discouraged, as parents can be ruined by it, as my parents were.

I love to see Indian films and at one time many were shown in special cinemas here, but now so many Indians have videos we see them at home. Vilma has them on her video every day and I often watch them with her. Some films are made specially for village people and I like these to remind me of home. One I saw recently had a village just like ours, but the story was very romantic and funny too. In it the hero, a very handsome man in the Air Force, marries a Brahmin girl, a caste above his, and refuses to take a dowry from her father who is a poor man. After their marriage he has to go to war and does not return, so they think he is dead. The young widow is nearly forced to marry a bad man because no other man would want to marry a widow, but she tries to take poison instead. The hero returns just in time to save her. In this way films are made to persuade people to change the old customs that are harmful. Most educated people have already done so. In the villages things change very slowly, and indeed there are still many things there that are beautiful and bring happiness and these I miss in my life here.

5

I have said that there were few really poor people in the village, apart from the Harijans, for ours is a rich state, with so many crops, wheat, maize, millet, sugar cane, and fruit and vegetables. However I did know one very poor couple who lived in a house in a nearby street. This house belonged to another of my aunts, the one whose husband went to Canada, became rich and never sent for my father. She had her own home here too; it was very fine, one of the best in the village. She had a modern kitchen, a flush toilet, beautiful furniture, and a dinner and tea set in china (ours were made of metal). Her husband never sent for her either, and they died without seeing each other again. Perhaps he was too mean to send the fare, for in spite of all their wealth they were noted for their meanness. If anyone gave my aunt sweets or cakes she would keep them until they were mouldy, and only then would she offer them to a visitor. We knew that we would be sick if we ate anything in her house.

This poor couple paid very little rent as their house was in a very bad condition, but they had nothing in the way of possessions, not a pot or pan or dish or any bed linen. I felt sorry for them; I had never seen anyone so poor before, so I kept taking food and dishes and clothes from home to give them in secret. I was often in trouble for giving our food and goods away to those I thought needed them. The woman was grateful and would do anything for me. We would sit together on the roof and she would massage my back or arrange my hair. Indian women often do this as it is so comforting. After a while they had a little son, and when he was about six months old the woman went to my aunty in great distress, crying and wailing. She said her husband had arranged to sell her and her child to a farmer and was going to return to his home town. My aunty took a big stick and went to their house; she shook it at him and threatened him so that he went away and was never seen again. The poor woman stayed in the house and brought up her child, getting a living by helping my aunt and other women in the house.

Selling one's wife is thought very shocking, but it is still done occasionally. Men do tend to think that their wives belong to them like possessions, and they are not considered to be men's equals. At the same time women are respected in their own place, which is the home, at least in theory. Some women prefer the certainty of marriage and children to having their freedom, when they may miss out on both. A woman with a good husband and enough money can live like a princess, with not too much to do and plenty of time to enjoy herself with her family and friends. As a bride she is very important; everyone is interested in her and pleased to see her as a visitor. Her happiness depends on her husband and his family, because after her marriage she belong to his family more than to her own. She will live in his parents' house and work for them. The mother-in-law looks forward to having a new daughter to do the work and give her a holiday. If she is spiteful, or thinks that the dowry was too small, or just happens to dislike the girl, she can make her life a misery. Sometimes brides kill themselves because of this; or worse, the husband or his parents find a way of killing her so that they can have another, better bride in the house. A good husband values his wife and depends on her. He is polite, does not take her sexual favours for granted, and gives her presents. If she has boy children she is more honoured.

The most terrible thing that can happen to a family is for an unmarried girl to have a lover and be disgraced in the eyes of the whole village. It is even worse if she becomes pregnant, for then there can be no doubt. Her whole family is disgraced, and not only will she be unable to marry, but her brothers and sisters will be rejected too. No one will speak to that family, do business with them, or give them work. Terrible things can happen. Sometimes the families lock themselves up in their houses and starve, ashamed to come out. Sometimes the girl will run away to the city without telling them and perhaps become a prostitute.

This is what happened to a friend of mine, Kamla, a few years older than me, while she was still at school. I used to admire and envy her and her sisters as they were quite well off and lived in the town. Kamla was always beautifully dressed, and she was clever at lessons too. Near the school was a temple, and Kamla used to go there, as many pupils do, to pray for success in her exams. But at this time Kamla became pregnant, and it was rumoured in town and village that one of these priests was the father. Then Kamla disappeared, and when we children asked about her we were told that she was dead. I heard the talk in the village; it was said that her parents had had her killed. There are doctors, it is said, who will give an injection to a pregnant girl that will kill her and then they will make out a certificate that says it was a natural death. The parents would have to pay a lot of money for this.

Naturally, when we young girls heard tales like this we were very frightened, but as a rule Indian men do respect us and never try to touch us if we do not encourage them. I did not know how girls became pregnant; nobody told me, and I had not the courage to ask. There was a family-planning clinic in our village, and there were posters for all to see. We children used to giggle about them, but I certainly did not know why; I just pretended to know, to seem grown-up.

There is one more sad tale I must tell of my own family. One of my cousins married a poor man and had four daughters, no sons. This was bad enough, but at sixteen the eldest daughter was found to be pregnant. The mother was in despair for her and for the other three daughters especially, so she got some poison and gave it to her daughter. Fortunately at that time a relative who had trained as a nurse was on a visit to their village and went to stay with them. Finding this girl very ill she asked the mother about her and heard the whole story. She was horrified. She took the girl to hospital where her life was saved, and then arranged for her to have an abortion, paying for it herself. Nothing is secret for long in an Indian village, and as usual the rumours got around, and this meant that it would be more difficult than ever to find a husband for her. The relative had to arrange this too, but the only man who would take her was a cripple, and very poor. Even he thought he was too good for her; he treated her badly and never let her forget her past.

I know my mother loved me dearly and she proved this many times, as you will hear, but I know that if I had become pregnant she too would have poisoned me.

6

One of my earliest memories is of the wedding of Indira, my second sister. The first was married before I can remember. How old I was then I do not know. We had no birth certificates or any other records to tell us, so people would remember a birth or a death by some special happening at the same time. I asked once when I was born and was told it was well remembered because everyone was so disappointed . . . I was the fifth girl in the family. My mother began to worry as soon as I was born about how she would find the money to marry me off! This was always the way in the village; to be unmarried was unthinkable. A woman without a husband was not a person at all. And this is how even a widow is considered. For the rest of her life after the death of her husband she is a person of no importance; she must dress simply in white or very pale colours, wear no jewellery or make-up, and of course she will usually be poor without a man to support her. If she has children she is of more account, and her relatives will probably help her more, but as a woman she is supposed to be finished, even if still young. Her relatives may try to find a man to marry her, and if they do, the ceremony is very small, with no rejoicing. Even in death the widow is not honoured as others are, and has a very simple funeral. You can see from this how important it is for girls to get married; it is looked upon as the most important thing in their lives.

Unless they are wealthy, the parents must sacrifice themselves for their daughters, providing them with dowries and paying for the wedding feast. It is also a great responsibility for them as their daughter's happiness and well-being depend on the parents being able to make a good choice. All village marriages are arranged and much bargaining takes place. Everything must be weighed up carefully. Are the young people of the right caste, are they matched in education, in their families' wealth and respectability, in looks and health, in personality and ability? Opinions are asked for all around, and secret investigations made, for who knows if the other side is telling the truth? Of course however careful the parents are there is still a lot of luck in it, for whether marriages are arranged or left to choice, as in this country, there is no way of being certain how it will turn out.

Once the parents have agreed, the wedding preparations can start. It becomes a time of excitement, hope and happiness, even if it is a great worry to the family concerned. They know that they will in turn be able to enjoy the many weddings of their relatives and friends, all through their lives, and this makes the effort even more worthwhile. A month before the wedding, relatives and friends come around to help. A tailor is employed to make new clothes for all the family and for the in-laws too. The bride must have a beautiful wedding sari in bright red and gold, and many more to take away with her. Even a poor girl should have ten at least, and a rich girl might have a hundred, some made of silk and embroidered by hand. There is a goldsmith in the village and the bride visits him to choose her jewellery, as she must have some gold for her wedding. This gold, though, is not pure, and like our silver has other metal in it, so it is not as expensive as purer gold would be. She can ask for special designs to her own taste, and is expected to have a necklace and earrings at the very least. If she comes of a rich family she will also have rings, bangles, anklets, nose jewellery, and ornaments for the hair and the hands, some set with precious stones. Meanwhile, preparations for the feasts and parties are going on, and these are considerable – as, for instance, when Indira was married we had two hundred guests, some from the groom's side, some from ours. Many came from distant villages and had to be put up for two nights at least, and fed too, very generously. It was no wonder Mother had to go to the village moneylender and pay back for so many years.

A week before the wedding relatives and friends of the bride come every day to dance and sing and play instruments in her home. She cannot join in, but she can enjoy all the excitement and anticipation. She has never before had such rich and beautiful saris and jewels, make-up and perfume to wear, nor has she ever been so important. Of course she must wonder about her husband, especially if he comes from a distant village and she does not know him, even by sight. And of course she learns all she can about him from her family and friends, and hopes she will fall in love as soon as she sees him. Then three days before the wedding there is a special custom, the same for the bride and groom, but kept separate. Friends and relatives come to their houses bringing rice which is boiled and eaten with milk and sugar or with brown lentils, to bring good luck. Then bride and groom are bathed and their faces and limbs are rubbed with 'manya', a preparation of oil and turmeric and other spices to make their skin smooth and beautiful.

The night before the wedding, they see each other for the first time, though only for a moment. The groom comes to the bride's door and she will have made herself as pretty as she can, putting on one of her new saris and doing her hair in a becoming style. She opens the door to him and he brings a garland of gold and silver flowers to place round her neck. She has another garland of gold and silver flowers for him. This is very romantic, especially if they like the look of each other.

Our guests were to sleep on mats on the floor in the house and his were to have the village hall. I remember we borrowed a quilt, pillow and sheet for each guest from our neighbours, and these were lent willingly as it is everyone's duty to help with a wedding. The bridegroom's family must also do some preparation. The groom must have new clothes; if he is rich these may be very splendid, but if he is poor he must at least have a good suit, a gold ring and a watch. He must bring a few especially fine saris for his bride and some expensive jewellery. When he comes to the wedding he should ride in a car decorated with flowers, or on a horse also decorated. His family comes too and they are accompanied by musicians and dancers who will play and sing and amuse the company for perhaps several days. You can see that everything is done to make our weddings beautiful and full of colour and romance. Everyone rejoices, and even if life is hard afterwards there is something wonderful to remember. I always thought I should have a wedding like this, and like most girls I used to dream about it and picture it in my mind. All these years later I sometimes imagine myself in such a dream, as my own wedding was so different.

You may be surprised to hear that our wedding ceremony takes place at three o'clock in the morning, so no one gets any sleep that night. The last preparations for the feast will be made at this time. The house will be made ready for the priest who will be coming to celebrate the wedding, and for all the guests. In the centre of the main room a special fire is lit; the wood for this is scented and sprinkled with ghee, which is clarified butter. Bride and groom stand close together so that her sari can be tied to his waist sash, signifying that they are now united. Then, with him leading, they circle around the fire seven times while the priest says prayers, stopping briefly after each circle is made. These prayers are in Sanscrit, which only the Brahmins know, so I have never understood what is said. When this is finished the man and the woman are a married couple, but they do not kiss each other as people do here. Bride and groom then separate and walk around the village or by the canals with their guests, and everyone wishes to see them and talk to them.

One reason I remember my sister's wedding so well was because there was a terrible storm that night and my family was very worried. The wind blew and the rain fell, and what was to be done with all the guests and the feasting if the weather did not change? Because of course, with so many people coming, the party must be in the open, and most of the cooking too. Already the wood was wet and the fires might not catch. Fortunately in the morning it was soon warm and sunny and all went well. Some of the men dug a big hole in the courtyard and lined it with fuel. It was lit well in advance so that it was nice and hot, and then a grid was placed over it so that the big pots of curry that had been prepared could be cooked. Another hole was dug in the same way to make a stove for the chapatis. There would be hundreds of these, all made by the women, for on this occasion men cooked the curries. There would be many different kinds of these, all specially delicious, as well as wonderful sweets, much better than the usual ones. My favourite was called peneen; it is made of milk and lemon juice strained through muslin, pressed and cut into strips and deep fried. It is served with curried green peas. People in this country who only know Indian cooking from take-aways do not realise that our food at home can be so good, when skilfully done with fresh ingredients, and cooked and eaten in the open air.

Village folk did not often drink alcohol, at least when I was a child, but weddings are different; then most of the men drink what is called 'real sherab', a sort of wine made secretly by the farmers and sold specially for weddings. Soon everyone is eating and drinking as much as they could possibly want and the courtyard is alive with bright colours, music and talk. Children get madly excited and run around, and soon the dancing starts, to go on for hours. The bride and groom sit quietly, they do not dance and sing.

You may wonder how my parents could pay for all this, even with the help of the money-lender. Fortunately my mother's brother paid for the main feast, and this often happens. When parents die everything is left to the males in the family, but it is understood that they should help their sisters with their children's weddings. I have been told that there is a law now that girls must inherit too, but as often occurs in the village laws are not taken too seriously.

Next day the guests must be fed again, and in some cases they may stay for a week or more. And there are two more little rites for bride and groom after the wedding. Each has a scarlet thread, knotted many times, made into a bracelet and put on the wrist, and she must undo his and he hers. The knots are very tight and hard to untie, and if they do not know each other and feel shy it makes them used to touching each other and sharing a task. It is meant to remind them that there are many knotty problems to come in married life which they should help each other to overcome. Then a tub of water is brought in and they sit beside it. A woman throws in a coin and they must compete to get it first. They are bound to laugh and struggle to win and this breaks the tension between them. This is done several times, and it is said that the one who wins will be the one to rule, but sometimes if the girl wins she will give the coin to her husband to save his pride and show she does not want to be the boss!

At last husband and wife are alone together. She is supposed to lose her virginity the first night, and their sheet should be stained with blood. This can be seen by the relatives next day, and if it cannot, whatever the cause, the girl will be disgraced and despised by her husband and both families, and everyone in the village will soon know. When I came to this country I learned that some innocent girls do not have intact hymens, so they suffer for nothing, but this is not generally accepted by Indians. I think we are certainly very ignorant about sex; I know I was when my turn to get married came. We would never have dared to ask our mothers to tell us, and even sisters and close friends never spoke about it. My eldest brother was different. I know this as I went to his wedding in Delhi and travelled back home with him and Sadesh in the train. All through the night he was talking to her very gently and getting to know her. Educated men like Krishna would not force themselves on their brides.

I do not know how Indira felt about her marriage, because even if she had spoken about it I was too young for such things. She was the last daughter to be married at home. The next day all the gifts and the dowry were on display in our house, and there were so many guests who all brought something, it must have looked very fine. There was more feasting and dancing that day, and on the next day my sister went to her new home with her husband's family. My uncle, as is the custom, carried her to the car, and as is also usual she took my second brother Veejay with her for company. As the new wife is going to live with people who are really strangers to her there is a custom that helps her to get used to them. On the second day in her new home some special biscuits are baked and put in a big bowl. She has to hand them round to each member of the family, several times. Then a special song is sung; it is called playing the Gori game, and it is sung to each relative in turn.

When Indira became pregnant she returned home to us. This is the usual thing to do, and is welcomed by many brides, who stay until the baby is born. Indira certainly seemed happy to be back. Later she went to England and I did not see her for many years.

7

My friend has asked me about my religion. It has always formed an important part of my life, so much that I breathed it in like air, without thinking about it. Just by our house was a temple, so that when there were festivals and many people came to take part they overflowed into our courtyard, and even into our front room, the doors of which were always kept open. They sat there all the time the services went on. My mother hated this, especially when men came from the temple and put loud-speakers up and the singing and playing went on till midnight. No one could sleep or rest or even talk!

In spite of how she felt, Mother had to respect the temple and the ceremonies, and she would often make tea and serve it to all who were sitting in and outside the house. Some members of my family were Sikhs. The men all kept their hair long and wore the turban. We were Hindus, but it seemed quite natural for us to go to this temple. I used to go every day when I was a child, just to sit and listen to the music and singing. There was another advantage, too: everyone who visits the temple is given something to eat, however often they go there. It is not very much, just a little semolina cooked in butter, or some fruit. This is like a blessing, and is also a reminder of a famous guru, whose story I will tell later. The temple is rather plain, just a big room with pictures of holy men on the walls and no statues of gods, but there are flowers, lights and incense, and music during the services. There is an altar there and on it is the holy book, the Granth Sahib, covered with gold scarves. This was written by the Guru Govind Singh, very long ago, at a time when the Moslems were persecuting the Sikhs and many died for their religion. The guru's father, his two sons and his wife were killed. We were told stories about him at school, and this is one of them as far as I can remember. The guru had many followers who believed in him, and to find the ones who had most faith he asked who would come forward and give up his head. Five came, and these men became his disciples. Of course he did not really mean to cut of their heads, but his followers thought he did. He called them all together and showed them a cloth covering what they thought would be dead bodies, but when he raised the cloth there was a great heap of semolina that had miraculously appeared. That is why the semolina is given to visitors to the temple.

Another guru, Nanak, wanted to convince the Moslems, who would pray only when they were facing towards Mecca, that God was everywhere, so it did not matter in which direction you prayed. So he went to a mosque and prostrated himself in prayer, but the whole temple revolved round so that his prayers went in all directions. Miracles like this made the Moslems revere him, and he is one of their holy men to this day. When he died he performed one last miracle to show people how to be peaceful together. Both Hindus and Moslems wanted his body, the Hindus in their fashion to burn it and the Moslems in theirs to bury it. Fighting broke out among them around where the guru's body lay under a shroud. Eventually someone pulled this shroud away and to their amazement the body had turned into a heap of beautiful flowers. The Hindus took half of them and burned them and the Moslems buried the other half. In this way they were reconciled.

The Hindu temple in the village was much bigger, a fine building with domes, and very rich inside with gold and colours. Here there were many statues of the gods; Shiva, Vishnu and Krishna I remember in particular. We used to visit this temple for special festivals and ceremonies. One of these is the name-giving for a new baby. If it is a boy there will be a party in the temple, and he will be dressed in white; if a girl, there is no party and a dark dress for her. The priest takes up the holy book and opens it at random; from the first word he reads he takes the first letter and this must be the initial letter of the child's name. There are so many festivals in the village and in the nearest town that there is always something going on. No one needs to feel left out; there is a chance for everyone to take part. If there is a wedding, for instance, all neighbours are welcome, and there are many opportunities to meet people and enjoy yourself. If you had time you could spend your life that way. These are things I miss in the UK.

The best festival of the year I thought was Devali, the feast of lights. Candles are lit everywhere, in the rooms, the windows, on the roofs, in the gardens. Even the graveyards are lit up with candles. If you go to the top of the house at night the whole village is a field of glittering stars. Delicious sweets are made and sent round to families and friends. Poor people come to the door and are given food. We all put on new clothes and go to the temple to honour Rama and Sita and rejoice that they have returned from the jungle. This is the story that was told to me.

Rama was a king's son, very strong and handsome and noble of spirit. There was another king who had a beautiful daughter called Sita who had been miraculously born when her father was ploughing, for she appeared as a baby in the furrow. When she grew up her father said that he would only give her in marriage to a man who could break a bow of iron. Many came and tried, but all failed until Rama came and succeeded and married the princess. Now Rama's father had another son by another wife, and she wished her son to be king when his father died instead of Rama, the rightful heir. She told Rama to go away to the jungle and stay there for fourteen years, and as he would not disobey her he agreed. Sita insisted on going with him and so did his brother Lacshman, so they all went and lived in the jungle. One day the two men went hunting and had to leave Sita alone. Rama drew a chalk line around the hut where they lived and told Sita she must not go outside it or let anyone come within it, but an old beggar man came and asked her for food and she took him in. This was really a very bad king called Raban in disguise, and as soon as he got his chance he seized Sita and took her away to his kingdom. Sita managed to drop some jewellery to show which way she had gone, and luckily Hanuman, the monkey god, had seen what had happened and followed them in the trees unseen.

When Rama and Lacshman returned and found Sita gone they were very sad and very angry. Hanuman told them where she was, so they raised an army to fight Raban. Sita was imprisoned in his palace because she would not give in to him, but Rama and Lacshman defeated Raban and killed him and Sita was saved. Then they returned home as the fourteen years were over, and found the old king had died, Rama's mother was blind from too much weeping, and the brother at home had never agreed to become king in Rama's place. He had placed a pair of Rama's slippers on the throne and worshipped them. That is why we celebrate Devali. The only sad thing I thought was that Rama did not take Sita back; he would not forgive her for disobeying him. I was glad, though, that I had been called after her.

Because Rama killed Raban, who was a sort of demon, there is another feast rejoicing in his death. Every year at this time an enormous image of Raban is made out of wood and cloth and paper, and painted in the brightest colours. He looks very fearsome and has many heads and arms, and is about twenty feet high. In the town near us, the figure was put up in the football ground and people came from far around to set up stalls selling food and drink and goods of every kind. Every night for a month there are plays put on in an outdoor theatre, showing different parts of the lives of Rama and Sita. There is a stage and red curtains at front and back. When the actors are on the stage someone behind the curtain speaks the words and they repeat them. To show the jungle, whole trees are brought on the stage, and fruit is hung on them. To amuse the crowd Hanuman the monkey god climbs up the trees and throws bananas to them. The actors are just ordinary people who often play the same parts year after year and become very good at it. A cousin of mine was very good at acting and singing and used to play the part of Sita, wearing women's clothes and a wig, and speaking in a high voice. Women do not often appear on the stage. We all enjoyed the plays very much, and there was nothing to pay, as all the work is done for nothing. At the end of the month the big figure of Raban is burned in a great bonfire.

Another festival that children like especially is called 'Holy' as it is a time when people throw coloured powder or dye over each other. They prepare bowls and buckets and watering cans full of red, yellow, green, blue, or any other colour, and if anyone comes to the door they get a big surprise. Some stay in all day and will not open the door, but really no harm is done because the colour washes off easily. You are supposed to keep it on all day, so anyone who has to go out to work or shop or go to school looks very funny. I liked Besantpanchani, too, when one must put on yellow clothes for the day and the village is as bright as a flower garden with yellow turbans, saris, tunics and scarves.

Between the Sikh religion and the Hindu, with all the different celebrations and festivals, I am quite confused and know very little, and I do not think I am unusual in this. What I do know is from the teachings of our guru, the Baba Charon Singh Maharaj. There were others in the same sect in the village and we would meet them in various houses to listen to the prayers and teachings. He tells us there is only one God, Parmatma, and the others like Shiva and Vishnu and the rest were not gods but holy men. The guru is the messenger of God and we must listen to him and obey him; if we do not we will be punished when we die. It is very important that we do not kill or eat any living creatures because when we die we will be born again, perhaps as animals if we have not led good lives. Every person has eighty-four reincarnations, the last ones most likely to be in human form, but if by then you have not learned to live a good life you will have to start again and do another eighty-four.

The way to live a good life is not to steal or cheat or lie, but that is not enough. You must get in touch with the God within you by meditating and listening for his voice, and you should do this for two and a half hours a day. I have never eaten meat or fish, or eggs, nor do I smoke or take more than a little wine occasionally, as is allowed on a social occasion; but the meditation I cannot manage, as my thoughts wander so much. The guru has many followers, all over the world; there are also some in Leicester, among them white people. In India he has a whole village where those who wish to learn from him can go and stay, for all their lives if they wish. Poor people do not have to pay, but are given their food and a place to stay because his wealthy followers give donations. There is also a hospital in this village and a school and everything that people need. The way of life there is simple, as the guru believes that we should not desire the things of this world, for this causes us to be unhappy and disappointed. When you are formally accepted as a member of his sect you are given a holy name by the guru himself. This happened to me in London when the guru was visiting the UK. My holy name is a secret I can tell no one.

8

I was fairly happy as a little girl, although I wished my mother was not away so much. My brother Krishna kept the family together and kept us in order too, though I did not appreciate it at the time. My two sisters Prem and Asha were still at home. Veejay was mostly in a big missionary hospital, where he was very well treated, although they did not manage to cure him properly. He would come home for holidays, and although often in pain he would play with us and read us stories from the books he had been given in hospital, and sing songs, Christian hymns he had learned, which we enjoyed.

I went to school in the village when I was about five. We learned to read and write in our local tongue, the language we speak at home, and in the language which is spoken more in the towns. We also did arithmetic and sewing. I did my lessons well and liked being in school. All my older sisters and brothers were clever, though only Krishna went to the university; perhaps I was not as bright as them, but I did well enough, and expected to get a good education. But by the time I was twelve and going to the secondary school things at home changed. Krishna had left and gone to work far away in Kashmir. Prem and Asha were living in hostels in town and studying at college, so I was very much alone, growing up with little help and guidance.

When I was thirteen I started my periods. My friend had told me when it had happened to her, but no one else had ever spoken of it, so I was very much in the dark. It first happened at school and I came home worried and frightened. Mother was home that day and was angry when she saw I had left school. 'Why have you come home like this?' she asked. I did not dare to tell her, but ran upstairs and stayed alone all day. I suppose she guessed but we never spoke ot it. I put some cotton stuff in my pants, as there were no sanitary towels in those days, but it was very uncomfortable and the blood often came through. This was a great worry to me. I soon found out that a menstruating woman is thought to be unclean and is not welcomed in her neighbours' houses as she will contaminate them. It is thought that food she touches may be poisonous and that she may cast a 'shadow' on children. I found this depressing.

All the same, the first year at secondary school was interesting. We started to learn English and geography and history, and I think that anything I know dates from that time. I loved my English teacher and would visit her in her house and help her, and it seemed I would do well like my brothers and sisters, but something went wrong with me. Looking back, I think I felt very unloved and unvalued at that time, and I also had the idea that I was different from other people. It was not because I believed I was cleverer or more beautiful than other girls, I just felt strange, as if I did not belong where I was. When I went to visit Prem and Asha in their hostel in the town I loved it and longed to stay there. Although it was not allowed, they used to keep me there in secret sometimes. Prem began to work as a nurse in the local missionary hospital and I used to visit her there. Some of the staff were white people, and I had only seen them once before. In fact the first time I saw them it made a deep impression on me. We were in class one day when the teacher told us that some white people were walking along the street, so we stood up on chairs at the windows to look out. A group of young girls, most of them with blonde hair and very fair complexions, were quite near us and we stared at them fascinated. I thought they looked like angels. When I saw the white nurses I was also drawn to them; my one ambition was to become a nurse and wear the uniform and be like them.

A year passed by; I was fourteen, and suddenly my whole life changed. I fell in love. Instead of learning in school I was in a dream all day, and at home I did little but play and try on clothes and do my hair. I told no one, but I could think of little else but a young man called Rama, who had come to the village to live with his aunt, who was one of my cousins. He was much older than I was, about twenty-four, unmarried still, and an engineer working in a neighbouring town. As he was a relative and I knew his sister Vina very well, I had every excuse to go there and see him as often as I wanted. I would go every day just to be near him, listen to him, look at him, and make his tea. While he was away, I would even go up to the room where he slept, to look at his clothes and touch them. I knew nothing about sex, my love was innocent and ideal, but it was very strong, as first love so often is.

Rama was very good-looking, tall, slender and always well dressed in a suit with shirt and tie, European style, and I was impressed with this. He was kind and friendly to me, would tease and laugh at me, and help me with my homework. He must have guessed how I felt about him, because everyone started to notice it, and the talk went round the village. I used to dream that some day he would marry me; the age gap would not be considered too great, and some girls do marry very young. What I did not realise was that he was too closely related to me to be able to marry me, but all the grown-ups would have known. Nobody said anything, yet I knew I should not be behaving this way. I just could not stop myself. Mother was so worried she began to come back early from her work to see what I was doing. She forbade me to go to his house, and when she noticed that I would sit up on the roof for hours in the chance of seeing him she would call me down. It was so strange that she never said anything direct to me. In spite of the love she had for her children she did not know how to talk to them, and this is quite common with Indian families.

Although Mother was always busy and over-worked she was very concerned for our welfare. After Indira had married and gone to England she began to think about a husband for Prem, who was at this time about twenty and had nearly finished her training. My parents had already spent a great deal of money on us: two daughters married at home,

Krishna put through university, Veejay treated in hospital, and three of us still to keep, including me still at school. They had heard that there were Indian men in the UK who wanted Indian wives and would not expect a big wedding and a dowry; they would even pay the fare to Britain. Village people think that everyone in the UK is well off, as they hear many stories about those who settle there and come back with lots of money and fine clothes and possessions. No one can starve in Britain; schools and hospitals are free and it all sounds wonderful. In fact as my parents were still in debt it was probably the only way they could marry off Prem. Indira, already in London, could help them. So in due course a husband was found for Prem and she went off in the plane alone to meet his family in London. It was not so very bad for Prem as she spoke good English, knew many British people, and as a trained nurse was able to look after herself.

Prem's marriage seemed to be all right, so then it was Asha's turn. 'Why not do the same for her?' thought Mother. Do not imagine that Mother wanted to part with her girls: it was dreadful for her to send them far away. But the power of the custom to get girls married is so strong it overcomes everything, and you must add to this the mother's fear that in India they would be very poor if they did get a husband. Any man willing to marry a girl with a very small dowry is bound to be poor himself; uneducated, perhaps in bad health and probably with little chance of improving his position. Survival must come first! Asha was my favourite sister, and the nearest to me in age. She would often bring me presents of dresses or ornaments from town, and we were happy in each other's company. I admired her for her cleverness and her good looks, and I thought of her as being very superior to me. The three years difference in age seemed a lot at this time. We were rather alike in appearance in those days, but I felt that I was compared unfavourably with her, and in spite of loving her I was jealous. It is only recently that I have been told by my white friends that I am beautiful, and because of this, as I shall tell later, have become much more confident. At that time I had very little confidence about myself in any way. This may have contributed to my desire for love from

Rama, and my obsession for him. It became so marked that Mother must have feared that I might get pregnant by a man I could never marry, and decided to do something drastic to prevent it.

Enquiries had already been made for a husband in Britain suitable for Asha. Indians, particularly the women, keep in touch with a very wide circle of relatives and friends, not only in India, but in Britain and other countries, and there is an endless interest in matchmaking. Mother heard of a family from our area who had a restaurant in London, and one of their sons was in his early twenties and unmarried. She began to negotiate on Asha's behalf, but as my behaviour became more and more worrying she decided that the same young man would do for me instead, and this would get me out of temptation's way. I do not remember that anything was said to me directly, but I heard my family talking of a marriage for me, and when I was quite sure that I was to be sent away I was horrified and heart-broken. I rushed out to Vina's house to see Rama, but learned that he had suddenly gone away. All the village knew that I was to be married and sent away, and Rama had left. Could it be for that reason? I decided I must see him again.

Next day I did a very bold thing. Without telling anyone I took a bus into town and then another to the village where Rama's father and mother lived. It took a long time, but when I arrived I found he was not there. His parents, being relations, were kind to me, gave me a meal and said I must stay the night. Rama was visiting the college in town, they said, and his father agreed to take me to see him next day. And so he did. Rama was playing tennis when we called; he was astonished to see me, and I burst into tears and cried on his shoulder. When we were left alone together for a while he comforted me and promised that he would come to see me in London when I was married. He seemed sad and distressed, and when we said goodbye he took me in his arms and held me tight. I still remember this vividly, and although I was never to see him again, I still love him in my heart.

9

I left Rama and returned home. I did not even care that everyone would be angry because of what I had done, and made them anxious when I stayed away all night and ruined my reputation. I felt nothing mattered any more. It was a turning point in my life, nothing was ever the same again. The first thing I was asked, of course, was, 'Where have you been? What have you done?' Then I felt frightened and lied. I said I had been to town to stay with one of my aunts. Even if this had been true it was bad enough, to go away like that, telling no one and staying the night, but of course Mother made enquiries and in time the whole truth was known. My parents, my family, all my relatives and friends treated me like a criminal. Soon everybody in the village seemed to know. I was a bad loose girl who went running after men, and who knew what I would do next?

By now my mother was hearing bad things about Nirmal, the man I was to marry. His brother came to visit us and let out that Nirmal drank and gambled, though he said in excuse for him that this was only because he was unsettled, being single, and would be quite different when he had a wife. He also had no job and no training, but his brother promised to give him work in the family restaurant where he was in charge. Then my sister Prem wrote to warn Mother against him. 'You should kill Sita rather than let her go to him', she said. Yet my mother did not want to believe it and the arrangements for my engagement went on. Nirmal's mother was a widow who lived in a village some distance away. She was very keen on the marriage. Meanwhile I was feeling very strange. I did not want to eat or to talk to anyone;

I did not care how I looked, and I went thin and pale. Strangest of all, I felt compelled to eat little pieces of clay that I took from the outer walls of the house. My mother realised that I was in a disturbed state of mind and she became frightened for me. Suddenly she changed her mind. She could not let me go away after all. 'I will stop the marriage, and you can stay at home', she said.

You might think that I would have been very happy to have been told this, but by now it was too late. I felt I could not possibly stay in the village or even in my own home, hated and despised. Nothing, I thought, could be worse than this. I must get away, anywhere else but here. When Mother realised that I could not be persuaded she told me I could stay with my sister Prem in Leeds, or Indira in London, and if I did not like Nirmal when I met him I could wait there until another match could be found for me. The law in England said that if you went there to marry a man you could stay for three months, but if you did not marry him then you had to go home. This would give me time to find out the best thing to do, and my sisters would help me. It did not seem so bad after all, and my new mother-in-law-to-be came to visit us with her daughters. I was disappointed as she was dark-faced and ugly and so were her daughters, but they were kind and friendly to me, which was a change, and if they knew any bad things about me they did not show it.

A day was fixed for the engagement, when there would be a party as for a wedding. Mother and I went to the city with one of her sisters who knew the shops there, and we bought ten fine saris. I did enjoy choosing the colours, mostly pale ones in pink, blue and green. Later I went to the goldsmith and chose my necklace and earrings. My parents had to buy many other things; Nirmal's measurements were sent and a three-piece suit was tailored for him. Another was made for his brother, and for Nirmal again, a watch and a ring. Saris had also to be bought to give to his mother, his sisters and his brother's wife. Then his mother sent me my wedding sari in red and gold, but it was of the cheapest kind, not nice at all. There was some good jewellery for me, but as I found out later it was borrowed and had to be given back. She also gave me two tunics and trousers and four saris, but these also were not good ones, or to my taste.

The engagement day came. I wore my red sari and the jewellery, there was a big party with music and dancing, but I enjoyed none of it; I just felt exhausted and helpless. The guests stayed the night and the next day I went with Fula, as my mother-in-law was called, to stay with some of her relations who lived in a village not far from Amritsar. Every engaged girl should go to the Golden Temple there to bathe in the sacred waters surrounding it. I could not help feeling happier when I saw this very beautiful place, true gold inside and out. Although a Sikh temple, Hindus visit it and reverence it as much as Sikhs do. I bathed there and prayed and made offerings.

When we returned home it was soon time for me to go. Nirmal's brother had agreed to pay my fare to London. My parents had a passport for me, and about this a strange thing was done. I told you that village people do not have certificates of birth, so there is no proof of when they were born. I knew I had been born in 1958. It was then June 1974, and I had turned fifteen in May. Everyone knew that I was too young to be married according to law in England, so it was decided to put some years on to my age. Mother thought that I would be more respected if I was thought to be much older, so she put that I had been born six years earlier, and was now twenty-one! In fact it worked the other way because my new relatives thought I was very stupid and ignorant for my age!

One morning, with my case packed and everything ready, I went with Mother and the travel agent to Delhi to take the plane. When it came to the point of leaving my home and family my indifference broke down, the reality suddenly hit me, and I suffered very much in saying goodbye. When I had to part with my mother it was far worse. We clung together, crying and crying. Then I was on the plane and alone.

10

I suppose anyone going in a big plane for the first time is very frightened and I was, of course; but I was more frightened by the strangeness of being in a different world, all by myself for the first time in my life. There were some Indians on board, including the man sitting beside me, but I dared not speak or even move. Some of the airline staff spoke in my language, but I was confused and seemed to understand nothing. I was given a drink of some kind, mineral water perhaps, but it tasted horrible to me. Then a tray of food appeared, but it was so strange I dared not eat it, as it might have been forbidden to me. Looking back I think it was fish and chips, which would have been. About two hours later the plane turned round and headed back to Delhi, as there was some trouble with the engine. We landed safely and were taken to a hotel. As it was very late we were given no food and I was almost too hungry to sleep. In the morning breakfast must have been served, but no one told me about it, or where to go, so I missed that too. Then it was back to the aircraft and we set off once more.

I had not been sitting there long when I realised that I had started a period, about two weeks early. This must have been because of all the fear and worry I had had. Too terrified to move, I just sat there. More strange food was offered, but by then I was past eating. I realised that there was a toilet on the plane, but I was too scared to get up, and it never occurred to me to ask one of the stewardesses to help me. Most people were speaking English, and although I had learned some at school I understood only a little. I felt such shame, misery and fear as I sat there hour after hour that I would have been very glad to have died.

When we arrived at the airport I covered myself with a big shawl that fortunately I had with me, so that if my clothes were stained it would be hidden. I knew that I must wait for my new relatives and my sisters to call for me, but first I had a medical examination. A doctor listened to my chest and took an x-ray, and although the medical people were quite kind in the way they treated me, they did not talk to me, nor did I to them. I dared not tell them about my period. Then I was left to wait in the lounge for someone to fetch me, but hours passed and no one came. Suddenly, to my relief, an Englishman appeared and told me that my relatives had been there the day before, and learning that the plane was delayed had returned home. Eventually I was taken in a car to a hostel where I was put in a nice room and able to have a bath. I washed my clothes and dried them as best I could as I had no change of clothes with me, only an overnight bag. Because we had been given food on the plane we were not given any more that night, so I fasted once more. Next morning there was breakfast and I drank tea and tried some cornflakes, but as I put plenty of salt on them they were not very nice.

Later that morning Nirmal and his brother and his wife came. My sisters were not there, to my surprise. The police had been to see my relatives to tell them that I had arrived the day before. As soon as I saw Nirmal I felt miserable. He was short and fat, with a dark face, which I have never liked, perhaps because my complexion is fair for an Indian, more like a dark European. His features were quite good, but his teeth were yellow and he was smoking all the time, another thing that is forbidden to our sect. I tried not to look at him, and spoke to his brother, the one I had met in India and thought pleasant, and to his wife. As we travelled to London and their home I thought, 'I will never marry that man!'

11

That June day was sunny and the sky was blue, and to London people I suppose it was hot, but to me it was delightfully cool. We had been roasting in Delhi, and I had been bitten badly by mosquitoes that summer, so the freshness was very welcome to me. We went by car to Southall and I was pleasantly surprised by their home which, as I realised later, was in a council housing estate. My new brother Anuz, his wife Nimmo, and their four children had a big flat in a clean new block, and the decorations and furniture were the best I had ever seen. I was particularly impressed by the carpet in the lounge; it was as blue as the sky.

When we arrived many of their friends and relatives had gathered to meet me. Although tired and hungry I was glad to see them and feel welcome. I heard people say 'Nirmal is a lucky fellow, what a good-looking girl she is.' Only my sisters were not there and this worried me. The food was good and there was plenty of it, so I ate hungrily. Then I went early to bed, sharing with the eldest girl of twelve. Early next morning my sister-in-law told me that she would be going to work in their restaurant in future and that I must look after the house and the young children. The two elder daughters of twelve and eleven would be at school, the little boy at nursery school, but there was also a baby of two, still in nappies. There was no washing machine but she told me how to wash the nappies and other things. They had a very big fridge filled with food, including many prepared curries which needed only to be heated up, but I was to make the chapatis and the dahl. I hardly knew how to tell her that I had never done washing, cooking, or even housework before. My older sisters were too impatient to teach me, and found it easier and quicker to do it themselves. As for Mother, I suppose that as I was the youngest girl she was inclined to spoil me. Nimmo knew my age had been changed on my passport, but I did not like to tell her by how much, so I seemed childish and ignorant to her. She remarked sarcastically that I must come from a wealthy family, no doubt with plenty of servants, but here I was expected to work.

Of course I knew that a daughter-in-law is always expected to work for her new family, so I did not complain but decided to learn as quickly as I could to avoid being despised. It is the custom for the bride-to-be to cook her first meal for the family on her second day, but I could not, so Nimmo made chapatis and rice and Nirmal made a black bean dahl. I watched and tried to learn. In a few days I could at least do the essential things, I even cooked meat, which they all ate except me, and I hoped Nimmo would be pleased for me, especially as she was a distant cousin. Sadly I noticed that she became less nice to me as I improved, and I think she was jealous. She looked rather old and ill and did not bother to make herself look more attractive, while I was young and pretty. I heard later that shortly before this time she had been in hospital with hepatitis, and already she was pregnant with her fifth child. Anuz was good-looking and pleasant in his manners; he made plenty of money from the restaurant, and must have been a good businessman, although he had very little education. Unfortunately he was a great spendthrift, giving parties at home nearly every day, and passing his evenings drinking in the pub or gambling in clubs. He often went away for weekends or longer, taking friends with him and paying for them all to stay at good hotels, but he never took Nimmo or the children. Everyone, including his wife, knew that he had a girlfriend. He had dozens of expensive suits and shirts, and everything that went with them, while Nimmo had to be content with pieces of material left over from a factory nearby for her saris. She said nothing, because there was nothing she could do but put up with it.

Several days passed. I saw little of Nirmal and we seldom spoke, because, by custom, bride and groom should not be together in the same house at all. In any case he was only home for meals, working during the day and going to the pub in the evenings. One day he went out and bought me a hairbrush and comb, the only presents I ever had from him. Nimmo gave me an umbrella but it was no use to me because I never went out of the house. No one thought of showing me the district where I lived, let alone the great city of London! In fact I am still waiting and hoping to have the chance of seeing it. All day I was busy at home working; the washing-up alone, with a big family and so many visitors, kept me on my feet for hours until late at night, and my feet and ankles began to swell up and be painful. My happiest times were when I could play with the two eldest girls, so close to me in age. They were my dear friends, and always nice to me, but oh how different their lives were from mine! I was fond of the little ones too, but fortunately I did not have them all the time; a lady from upstairs used to look after them too.

Many of our visitors, I found, were the Indian girls and women working in a nearby factory which belonged to friends of the family. Then one day I was taken to see this factory, and to the family restaurant. It was big and rather dark and rich-looking. Nirmal was working there from early in the morning, doing odd jobs nearly all day and many evenings. For this he was paid only about twenty pounds a week and was very bitter about it, but Anuz said that as he was living at home with all expenses paid, it was worth much more. He may have been thinking that if he gave Nirmal a better salary he would drink and gamble it away, and though Anuz did this himself he at least could well afford it.

I still felt no attraction towards Nirmal, but for a time I thought I could not escape from marrying him, and perhaps it would not be too bad. We would live with Anuz, who was quite kind to me, and Nimmo, who at least did not harm me, and the children seemed like brothers and sisters to me. Nirmal would earn a good salary in time, so we would be quite well off and I would have more freedom after marriage. He could not treat me too badly in the midst of his own family. However, as time went on and he became more and more rude and bossy, I became more and more aware of disliking him. He would hand me his dirty washing, ordering me to wash it, and then complaining if it was not clean enough. I did not dare to tell him that his shirts and underwear were so old and worn and so ingrained with dirt that it was impossible to do better. Sometimes when he returned for lunch he refused to eat my cooking, shouted angrily at me, and even threw it in the bin. No one stood up for me and I became timid and withdrawn and lost all appetite. Nirmal would shout at me, 'Eat, eat. Why don't you eat!' I said nothing, and ate nothing. I had become too depressed, and I grew thin and pale.

At last one day my two sisters Indira and Prem came with their husbands to see me. I broke down and cried when they came in, and told them in front of everyone how unhappy I was, and how I did not want to marry Nirmal. I begged them to take me away with them. There was consternation! My relatives started to shout that I was being ill-treated; the others shouted back and soon everyone was quarrelling and angry. My relatives walked out and were told never to come back, but I thought they would soon be back to save me. In fact I never saw them again until my wedding day. Later I found out the reason why they acted as they did. They had told me and my mother that I would be staying with them before marriage, that I would have the chance to change my mind and that they would find another, better husband for me if necessary. But this was never meant, as Indira's husband was too poor to take me in, let alone pay for my wedding, and Prem's was too mean. None of them had the slightest intention of really helping me. All those promises had been made just to keep us quiet. What they wanted was to get me married and off my parents' hands, but knowing my mother's love for me they had deceived her. I learned also that exactly the same thing had been said to Mother about Prem when she came to London, but she was lucky, she had a good husband, even if he was mean, so she had not needed help.

After this meeting, and the fact that my sisters did not return, I realised with horror that I was all alone in a strange land whose language and ways I hardly knew, and with relatives who were now openly hostile to me. Nirmal had always known that I did not fancy him, and perhaps in spite of his bullying ways he had fancied me, but now that I had said openly what I thought of him he was angry and bitter and treated me with hatred and contempt. I went on working automatically, feeling more and more exhausted and unwell, too sad even to play with the children as I used to. I still went on saying I did not want to marry Nirmal, but I really knew I had no escape. They realised it too, but were still at bit anxious in case I did something desperate, as girls in my position sometimes do. That is why they made sure I did not see my sisters again, and why they never let me go out alone or even took me anywhere. The only times I did leave the house were once to visit some distant relations who lived in the next street, and to the friend's factory and the family restaurant with Nirmal. He wanted me to work there, but Anuz and Nimmo were angry as they wanted me to stay at home and do the work there. In fact Nimmo, who had never been able to go out and leave the children, was enjoying her freedom. She and her husband and Nirmal would go out to the films and to restaurants, leaving me behind.

Then Nirmal left the restaurant and was given a job in the factory. For a time I worked there part-time, but it was a nightmare. Nirmal showed me how to work the machine that did the button-holing but he was so impatient that he did not explain it properly, and I was too frightened to take it in. In front of all the girls, he lost his temper and struck me hard on the face, pulled my hair and punched my head. Some of the girls cried out in protest, but most of them did not dare interfere. Things were worse at home, too. Nimmo opened my trunk and saw the clothes, jewels and gifts that I had brought for my dowry and said they were rubbish. After my work at the factory where I did learn to use the machine at last, I had to start work at home, so I was always tired. Nirmal and Anuz were continually quarrelling and gradually, from what was said, and from what Nimmo told me because she could not resist complaining, I was able to find out a great deal about Nirmal. He was the only son of a second marriage and was very spoiled by his father, elder brother and sisters.

Unfortunately he turned out badly, and even as a child was a thief. In his teens he joined a gang of village boys who went around threatening shopkeepers with knives if they did not give them money, hiding their faces with scarves tied round them. He started to drink and gamble and was a terrible worry to his old parents. When Anuz went to England he made enough money from his restaurant to send for his family, including Nirmal, hoping to set him up in life. It had been a failure, as Nirmal never kept a job, left home and lived in rooms in the poorest areas, and spent what money he could get on drink, gambling and women. To get him married was their last hope. They could not expect to offer him anything but a poor dowryless girl whose parents were desperate, and I was to be sacrificed in a hopeless attempt to save him.

Some of this I may have learned later, I cannot be sure, but I knew enough to be even more reluctant. Noticing this, Anuz and Nimmo changed their tactics. They were nicer to me, and appealed to my family feeling. The wedding date had been fixed long before I had arrived. The hall had been booked, hundreds of invitations had been sent out. If I refused to go through with it, think of the shame I would bring to their family and my own. They even went down on their knees before me, nearly crying! Anuz said, 'You need not worry about Nirmal, I will be responsible for you, and insist that he treats you well. In my home you will be safe and happy.' This appeal worked on me much more strongly than their anger had, and besides, I believed Anuz, who had never been actively unkind and even seemed to like me. He was, after all, old enough to be my father. I gave in and agreed, and the preparations for the wedding could go ahead. It was only six weeks since I had come to London, but it seemed like six years.

12

A few days before the wedding I went to stay with the
relatives in the next street, as it would be unfitting for bride
and groom to be in the same house just before the marriage.
These people were kind to me. I kept quiet and did everything correctly. They gave me manya according to custom,
and many friends and relatives came each day to dance and
sing and eat together. To my disappointment the wedding
was to be a Sikh, not Hindu one, because although all the
preparations are the same, the actual ceremony is different.
There is no sacred fire lit for bride and groom to circle round.
One day I was told to get ready to go to an office to get the
marriage registered. I was dressed in my red and gold sari,
my hair was carefully arranged and my make-up beautifully
done, but I could take no pleasure in it. I looked in the mirror
and saw that I had lost some of my good looks in those few
weeks, but I did not care, my heart was too sad. My sisters
came that day and their husbands too; they had to be asked in
spite of the quarrel. When they saw how miserable I looked
they said, 'Don't worry, we will take you away if he is cruel to
you.' I no longer believed them. Anuz drove us to the office,
with Nimmo of course, and when we arrived met some of
their relatives. I was given a gold ring for Nirmal and he had
one for me. I do not remember much about the ceremony, it
was so strange, and as it was in English I did not understand
anything. It was almost the first time I had heard it spoken
since I arrived, and the little I had known seemed to have left
me. I mechanically did what I was told, stood beside Nirmal
and repeated in English quite meaningless words. We exchanged rings, various things were said, and it was over. I did

not know then, or for a long time, that I was now Mrs Sagoo. Afterwards we went straight back home, nothing more was said; it was just an ordinary day.

On my real wedding day there was much more excitement. My hair was very carefully dressed; my face made up according to custom, and Nimmo gave me some really good jewellery. There was a necklace of heavy gold with fine stones, earrings to match, and bangles. When we got to the hall there were about three hundred guests there. Nirmal came in a turban, smartly dressed, but I thought he looked ridiculous with his eyes outlined with kohl. There was a stage, and on it on a low table with the holy book adorned with many fine scarves embroidered with stars. All around were beautiful flowers. The guests put money, both silver and notes, on the stage for the temple.

I came in between my two sisters, as I had no father or brother to give me away. I was wearing a red tunic and trousers, the *salvar komise*, and the thin red veil covered my face, as they led me to the stage to sit before the holy table. Nirmal came and sat beside me, and someone tied the end of his big sash to my veil. Tied like this we circled round the table while the priest said the prayers, and in this way we were married. Trays of semolina were brought in and offered first to us and then to the guests. I was crying all the time under my veil, and so were my sisters. Brides often cry because they are leaving their parents and their homes for the first time, but I had already lost these. I was crying for myself and my future.

After this we all sat down at the long tables that had been prepared for the wedding feast. Nimmo was beside me and my sisters on the other side, but Nirmal was sitting somewhere else. There were many curries, dahl, rice and puris, served in deep trays. It is the custom for the bride to eat from the plate of her new relations to show that she is now one of the family, and Nimmo invited me to eat from her plate. Now before this, my sister Prem, who had trained as a nurse, had told me that I must never eat from Nimmo's plate as she had been so ill with hepatitis. Without thinking I refused, though of course I could have taken a little, just for this occasion.

Nimmo was deeply offended and told her husband that I had insulted her. He started to shout at me and Nimmo, who was crying by now, turned on my sisters and accused them of turning me away from her and her family. My sisters replied angrily, and then Nirmal joined in too. The wedding feast ended in misery as my sisters walked out in tears, and soon all the other guests went away. Nimmo was never friendly to me again, and never forgot.

I felt terrible through all this; as if the marriage was not bad enough without this! Actually I did not feel really married, as I am not a Sikh, and I was glad of it. What I did not realise was that the civil marriage that had taken place just before was the one that really counted.

13

When we arrived home there were many guests to receive us. Drinks were handed round to the men, and I realised that Nirmal, who must have been drinking before, was drunk. I left the lounge and went into the kitchenette, as no one had spoken to me and I realised that I was in disgrace. They all sympathised with Nimmo, who was telling them what an ungrateful girl I was after all they had done for me. There were some ladies I didn't know in the kitchenette eating some food, but they did not speak to me either. At about eight o'clock Nirmal sent Nimmo to tell me to go to bed in the new bedroom, but I said that I wanted to sleep in my old room with my little cousin. She asked me to go with her to the lounge and speak to Nirmal, but I would not. She went away, but soon came back to say that he was not in, so I went to the bedroom and sat on the bed in my tunic and trousers. It was such a dreary room! It had belonged to two of the children, and it was empty except for the bed, a chair and a wardrobe. It is customary to prepare the room for bride and groom with flowers and fruit and nice sweets and drinks, but Nimmo had not bothered. If I had been a girl from a rich family it would have been done, but I was worth little. The expenses they had had were for show, to impress friends and relations, not for me. Even the jewellery Nimmo had given me had been taken back. I was thinking of this sadly as I sat there. I did not know that there was anything else to marriage. The only time anything had been said to me was a few days before when a woman I hardly knew said, 'Take this little towel and put it beside your pillow on the first night of marriage. Do not be afraid, you have to do nothing.' I thought that perhaps the towel was for good luck, and I had it there.

Suddenly Nirmal came in, very cross and drunk. 'Are you going to sleep here or not?' he asked. I didn't answer, I felt very frightened. 'Very well,' he said and went and locked the door. 'Now take off your clothes'. I sat there saying nothing, but I shook my head. Without another word he rushed at me and started to pull at my clothes, but I screamed and tried to defend myself. This made him go wild; he tore at them until I was naked, and although I fought him, thinking he had gone mad, he tired me out and threw me on to the bed. He forced my legs apart, and I felt a great pain. Almost immediately blood flowed out of me; I felt its warmth, and suddenly Nirmal stopped, put on his trousers and, without a word, ran out of the room.

I lay there crying hysterically, bewildered at what had happened, so much worse than anything I could have possibly imagined. I was bruised, bitten and scratched. I knew now what the towel had been for, but it was too late, the bed was badly stained with blood. Soon after, the door opened and Nimmo came in. I heard later that the adult members of the family had been listening outside the door. It wasn't customary for the groom to run away on the wedding night, so she thought she should do something. It was something very strange. As she came in she started to clap. Perhaps it was to show that at least I had been a virgin and they were all pleased. She said, 'It's all right, this happens to all of us; it happened to me too.' I could only say, 'I want my mother, I want my mother, I want to go back home.' She went away, and I was alone. Nirmal did not return that night. I lay thinking and wondering what I could do. I wanted to run away, but where could I go? I knew now that my sisters would not help me, though perhaps they would like to; it was their husbands who would never let them. I thought I might take a knife from the kitchen next day, hide it in the bed, and if he came at me again I would kill him. I wondered what my poor mother would think if she knew what was happening to me. At last, exhausted, I fell asleep.

Next morning Nimmo came in again and told me to wash the sheets, so I put them in the bath and did as she said. They were a gift from my mother, and she had embroidered them herself. This made me even sadder. I returned to bed and lay there all day, without food or drink, and no one came near me. All day my thoughts were hard and bitter, towards Nirmal and his family, and my sisters for getting me in this position in which there seemed no hope. Another night passed, and Nirmal thankfully did not appear. Nimmo came in the morning and told me she would be going to the restaurant so I must get up and look after the children. I made them some food, and ate some myself. I was glad to have something to do and the company of the children.

In the evening Nirmal appeared. I thought he seemed less confident, although he told me to remember that I was his wife. 'And don't start screaming again; get me some food.' I was afraid he might hurt me if I did not, so I made him a meal. That night he came to the bedroom, but when I refused him he did not insist. Perhaps he had some respect for me because I had been a virgin, or perhaps he was tired out from the night before, as he told me later that he had gone straight out to stay with his girlfriend. Later I had to give in to him, but at least it did not hurt me, though I hated his sex and I hated him. Otherwise life went on much the same; I worked part-time at the factory as before, and did housework and cooking for most of the remaining time. I heard Nirmal quarrelling with Anuz, who didn't want me to work outside but to be useful at home, and would not help me get an insurance card. I didn't understand what this meant then, but I knew that my passport was very important because I'd been told this in India. Unfortunately Anuz had taken it from me when I arrived at the house, and I didn't see it again for a long time.

After what happened to me, I should like Indian girls who come over here as I did, knowing nothing, to have the chance of learning from my experience. My passport was only valid for three months; after that, if I did not marry, I would be an illegal immigrant. So on marriage it is necessary for the passport to be sent away to be stamped, and then you are free to stay for ever. My relatives never did this, so I had great difficulties later on. They must have done it on purpose because they knew all about rules and regulations in the UK.

It enabled them to say, as they often did, that I had no right to be here and that they could sent me back to India if they wanted. Of course I did have the right to stay, but I thought they might destroy the certificate and deny that I was married, sending me back home to bring shame and ruin on my family there. My sisters had told me that if I ever told Mother the truth about my life here it would kill her, so I wrote home saying I was well and happy. My English friend who is writing this down and who knows me and my story so well says that I could have proved my marriage, as records are kept in a special office in London. But she hasn't realised how helpless and ignorant I was. Although living in England, I was kept completely apart from English life and people, as if I were still in India, but without the protection of family and custom that I would have had there. Over here I was like a prisoner, alone among my own people.

There are many young girls, some no older than I was, still coming over to marry Indian men they have never seen. I feel this should not be allowed. Let the men choose girls who have been brought up here, have families who care, and have had an education. They are not so easy to put down. That is why the men want village girls who are ignorant and alone, who can be kept apart, never even speak the language properly, and dare not complain. In India husbands do not often drink and gamble heavily or beat their wives, and although there is no real equality, women are usually respected. If seems to me that something happens to some Indian men when they come here, they often go right down, and become horrible.

Meanwhile at home Nirmal was quarrelling more and more with Anuz. He seemed to be always in a rage, and turned it on me, hitting me with his hand or fist or kicking me for no reason. If I looked out of the window, or sat for a moment, he would shout at me and beat me. One day there was a party at our house, and it happened that one of the guests was an older lady who had been divorced. I had met her before and she was one of the few people who talked kindly to me. Nirmal told me not to speak with her again, as she was a bad woman, but I forgot his threats and did so. In front of everyone he knocked me over and started to kick me, even to beat me with his belt. Everyone was amazed, and some men pulled him away and took him out, but my relatives never tried to save me. Anuz's promise meant nothing, and I think Nimmo enjoyed watching the way Nirmal treated me. At the factory it was no better. I learned slowly, and as I was on piece-work earned very little. Perhaps I would have done better if I had not always been expecting a blow from Nirmal. I never saw the money I earned; in fact at this time I had never had a penny in my hand. He kept the money for his drinking, and in spite of their differences, he and Anuz would go out every evening to pubs and clubs, returning at midnight or after, and Nimmo and I had to stay up to give them their dinner. We were not to eat until they came, so we were not only tired but hungry.

When I was left alone in the house I would sometimes ring my sisters and tell them about my life, but they always said the same things: there was nothing to be done, but perhaps Nirmal would improve. They never came to see me or invited me to see them, and indeed it was a long time before I met them again. One day Nirmal told me to pack our bags as we were leaving the house. One of the girls at the factory had told me that he was in the habit of stealing the clothes and giving them to girls he met in the pub, so perhaps he was given the sack. At any rate he did not work at the factory again, but went on Social Security and took me to live in another part of Southall. There we had one room in a house owned by an Indian couple and there were several other families living as we did and sharing bathroom and kitchen. As before, Nirmal went out every day to the pub and came home late and drunk. I think he must have done some part-time work as he seemed to have money. I did not, of course, and was often without food. He would bring back a chicken or some lamb for me to cook, but I could not eat them so had only lentils and chapatis. I began to feel ill and sick and the landlady, who was kind, would bring me curries she had made. When she saw Nirmal hit me she would tell him to stop, and as he did not want to be told to leave he would wait until we were alone.

Although I didn't know it I was pregnant; it was three months since our marriage. The landlady took me to see an Indian doctor who told me, but when I told Nirmal it made no difference. I was still beaten and kicked, or strapped with his belt, and although everyone knew and tried to stop him, he was so violent and would come to blows with anyone who interfered with him, that he was left alone. I was taken to the ante-natal clinic where there were Indian-speaking nurses and doctors, but I did begin to remember my English better and to pick up some more. One day when I was six months pregnant I fainted while waiting there. I had been feeling ill all the time and was getting worse not better, so when I was told I must go to hospital I was glad. I had gone very thin and was so anaemic that I was given blood transfusions and put on a drip for about two weeks. The nurses were very kind and my health improved, but then unfortunately I had to go back home. I never told anyone there how I dreaded this. I could of course only speak a little English then, but I would not have dared to even if I could. In all the weeks I was in hospital neither Nirmal or any other relation ever came to see me. I went back with a heavy heart.

There was no change in Nirmal when I returned. I was still beaten and half-starved and dependent on the kind woman there for extra food and for sympathy. When my time came it was she who sent for the ambulance and took me to hospital. I had no idea what would happen to me as no one had told me what to expect.

14

In the hospital I felt safe, as the nurses and doctors were kind and gentle. As my pains got worse I was given injections that made me sleepy and confused, but did not suffer so much. I was twelve hours in labour, and towards the end I was crying and calling out; when the baby was born I was badly torn, and by then I was so tired I did not even want to see him. To tell the truth, I did not feel at all like a mother: that feeling came only gradually over the next few weeks, and what I wanted was to be comforted by my own mother. I was glad of course that I had given birth to a boy. This was something I could not be reproached for.

Nirmal did not come to see us right away – he was too busy celebrating the birth of his son with his friends, and when he did arrive he was drunk. He had chosen a name for the baby, a Sikh name, Hernaik, though I would have liked to call him by a Hindu name – Sunni perhaps. Next day I tried to feed my baby but the milk did not come; indeed I was never able to feed him properly at the breast. I had a good look at him and saw that he was a very handsome boy, with thick dark hair and big dark eyes. He was more like me than Nirmal, I was glad to see, though his skin was darker than mine. With more food, rest and kind treatment I began to feel stronger, and when Nirmal came again I defied him and said I would take my baby away and live without him if he treated me badly again. 'Just wait until you get home,' he said, 'I'll soon stop your mouth.' I had hoped that now I was the mother of a son I might be given some respect, or even that my sisters would come and take me home with them, but they never came to see me.

If I had spoken English I might have confided in the nurses or doctors, or known about the hospital social workers. You might think I could have spoken to the Indian staff, but I had already tried to get help from our GP. When I was pregnant I had told him how Nirmal was beating me and keeping me without food, but he seemed to be angry with me. 'If your husband ill-treats you, go to the police, and take him to court. It is no business of mine,' he said. I knew then that I would never get help from my own people. A woman should allow her husband to kill her rather than complain.

After two weeks Nirmal came one evening to take me home. I carried Hernaik and we went by bus. I found there was no food in the house, no baby clothes, no milk, cot, pram or nappies. Fortunately my landlady had sent me some old clothes and a few nappies. I tried to feed the baby but I had so little to give him that he cried and cried, and sucked so hard that my nipples were very sore. I had little sleep that night. Early next morning I asked Nirmal for some money and went out to buy milk. A cheque for twenty-five pounds had arrived for me, and I was hoping to spend it on things for the baby, but he insisted on going with me to the Post Office to cash it right away. That same night he went out and lost it all gambling. While he was away I rang Nimmo to tell her what was happening and to ask her to help me for the child's sake, but all she would say was, 'You must keep quiet and not complain. It will be all right in the end.' What end, I wondered. Will that be when I am dead? I now had the baby to think of as well as myself – how were we to survive?

Every day I found I loved the baby more, and as he was the only person in the world close to me I became obsessed with him, watching him anxiously all day and waking up again and again in the night to make sure he was well and comfortable. I did manage to get money to buy him milk and orange juice and rose-hip syrup as I had been told, and he grew big and strong, and very loving too. Fortunately Nirmal was not in much and took little interest in him. Fortunately, too, the other Indian women in the house were helpful, gave me food and advised me about the baby. This prevented me from feeling despair and hatred for all human beings, as I now hated my sisters and all my uncaring relations as well as Nirmal, whom I hated most of all. I took Hernaik to the temple one day, just to pray, make an offering, and feel that he was blessed. Nirmal would not come, so the landlord's son, who was nineteen, said he would go with us. People in the temple thought he was my husband, and we laughed at this, but I thought: if only he had been! No one could be as bad as Nirmal!

When Hernaik was about six months old, Nirmal began to notice him more, and would pick him up and play with him. But if he cried in the night or at any time that Nirmal was in, he would slap him on the face or hit his bottom and of course this made Hernaik cry more. The poor baby became frightened whenever his father appeared. At this time, too, Nirmal would sometimes put curry or even hot pickle in the baby's mouth while he was eating, in spite of his screams, saying he wanted him to get used to Indian food. I could not bear this and tried to stop him, but Nirmal beat me and kicked me, until the baby, already screaming, was wild with terror. He was to see me being beaten many times in the next few years, and I often wonder what effect it has had on him. He is a very reserved child now.

One night when Nirmal came home drunk he found fault with me as usual, and after hitting me with his fists he dragged me to the front door and pushed me out into the corridor, which was open to the street. I was dressed in tunic and trousers and the autumn night was cold. He locked the door and I stood there shivering. When I heard the baby cry I knocked and called to be let in but there was no answer. Had he fallen asleep or was he deliberately leaving me to freeze outside? I do not know. Hours passed – I felt sick and ill with cold, but it was only when light began to show in the sky that I heard him come to the door and open it. I was so cold I could hardly walk into the house. He did not speak and I could not. I stumbled in and went to my baby.

It seems strange to me now that I stood there alone and uncomplaining and asked no neighbour for help, especially as this was to happen again. Three times more I was punished in this way. Perhaps he hoped I would die of pneumonia, as might well have happened in the weak state I was in from ill-treatment and lack of proper food. Looking back I realise that when one is in a situation that everyone seems to accept as normal, one becomes 'brain-washed' into believing that it is, however terrible.

Nirmal and the landlord, who also beat his wife, used to go out drinking together, but they quarrelled too, and eventually after a bad quarrel we had to leave. We moved several times, until we found a small basement flat in Stepney that was very cheap to buy. Nirmal tried to borrow the money from Anuz, but he refused. I even went and pleaded with him, but he would not help. I suppose he knew that Nirmal would never pay him back. Eventually we took a room with an Indian couple, and to my delight the landlady, Seroye, was from my village. Her husband, Mr Beg, was a big strong man and when I spoke with his wife about Nirmal, she told him too. Mr Beg said he would not allow Nirmal to beat me in his house. He had once broken a man's arm because he would not stop beating his wife. Nirmal heard about this, and was careful not to let him see, but if he attacked me in the room, Mr Beg would hear, and shout through the door, telling him to stop or come out and fight. Even this did not save me. I was by this time three months pregnant – there is only eighteen months between my two sons – but this made no difference to Nirmal. In a rage once because I had bought an old piece of carpet for our room, he knelt on my stomach as I lay in bed and put his hands round my throat to choke me. I gave a loud terrified scream before he could stop me, and Mr Beg ran in and hit Nirmal so hard across the face that he let me go and rushed out of the house. I looked so ill and shocked that he and his wife sent for an ambulance and I was taken to hospital. I was kept there for a week and given injections, I never knew why, but then I had to return home. I was longing to see Hernaik, and anxious about him.

I hurried to the house, but when I got there Seroye told me that she had looked after the baby until Nirmal came one day and took him away. I guessed he had gone to his brother's house, so I ran to the bus and then all the way there. I rang the bell, and Nimmo came to the door with Hernaik in her arms. I held out my arms to take him but she stepped back and tried to close the door. I pushed against it and cried out demanding my baby. To my amazement Nimmo shouted that I was a bad woman who had run away to another man and left my husband and child. A number of her women friends appeared behind her, and they all looked at me with hostility. I was both frightened and angry. 'I was in hospital, you know I was,' I cried. 'Give me the child and I will go.' She drew back again, looking at her friends as if for support. I remembered then that I had for once had a visitor while I was in hospital, a distant cousin who wanted to see me before she went away. Nimmo was related to her too and would trust her. 'Ring up Milma,' I said, 'she came to the hospital. She will tell you the truth.' Nimmo went inside to ring up, and fortunately Milma was in and told her where I had been. Only then could I enter the flat and seize Hernaik and hug him. Even Anuz and Nimmo felt a little guilty after this; they had believed the lies that Nirmal had told them. They let me stay for three days.

I went home and found that we had to move as Nirmal had quarrelled again with the landlord. I was very sorry, for they had been good friends to me. As usual we took one room in an Indian household, and when he started to beat me as he usually did on most days, our neighbours were distressed and called the police. Two policemen came into the room and questioned Nirmal. I could not follow what they said, but from Nirmal's tone I gathered that he was saying it was not true, his neighbours were trying to make trouble for him. I was sitting on the bed. The policemen looked at me, but I turned my face away. Even if I had known the words I would have been too frightened to speak. Three times more during my pregnancy the neighbours called the police, but although Nirmal was taken to the police station on the next occasion they released him later. Then he was taken to court and fined, but it made no difference to me. In fact it was worse, as he hated me more, and the sympathy I had from the neighbours made him furious.

I have never been able to understand why he was so cruel to me. I never harmed anyone, and if he had been kind to me

I would have learned to love him. I think some people, and he was one of them, must be born evil, for it was not only to me that he was always doing harm but also to everyone he knew, unless they were drunkards and criminals like him. And why did my sisters not help me, at least a little? I was so young compared to them. While I've been speaking of this time I find myself crying; and when I stop I feel depressed for the rest of the day. My friend asks me if I want to go on, as she knows how it makes me suffer to remember those days, but I want it to be known that these things can happen to young Indian girls like me. I must go on.

15

The next six months passed slowly and painfully. This time I was to go to another hospital, because my sisters said that the last one was too far away for them to visit me, but if I went to a nearer one they would come. I had to get two buses to reach this hospital, where I went to the ante-natal clinic; it became very tiring for me as time went on. I started labour just after Christmas, and it was a bad time to go to hospital. Most of the staff were on holiday and there was an air of neglect about the place. If only I had been at the first hospital, I thought, where it was so comfortable and everyone so kind; and, after all, no one came to see me except Nirmal. One big relief though was that I was not so worried about Hernaik as an Indian nurse at the clinic had told me how to get him taken into care.

This time the birth was much easier. Little Koldeep was smaller than his brother had been, had the same black hair and skin a little darker than mine, but his eyes were smaller and rather slanty like his father's. He was a delicate baby, and was to cause me much anxiety over his health. It was a pity that I was again unable to feed him at the breast, probably because I had not been properly fed since I had come to Britain. I was seventeen.

This time Nirmal actually came the next day and brought me some fruit. To have two sons one after the other is considered very lucky by Indians, and the mother is usually honoured for it. I also had another visitor who was very welcome: my sister Asha who had come over to be married. She was now twenty-one and had completed her studies to be a secretary, so Mother had arranged for her to marry a man in Leicester. It was lucky for her that she had missed being married to Nirmal instead of me, but she too was to have great difficulties. When Asha arrived at the airport, Jasvinder, her intended husband, came to meet her with his family and she went with them to Leicester. She did not see him again for some time, as apparently he now refused to marry her. Later she found out why. He had been living for some years with a half-caste girl, to the great annoyance of his family. They kept working on him to marry an Indian girl, and at last he agreed. When he told his girlfriend this she was very upset, for he had recently agreed to marry her and she had even bought the wedding dress. So, before he left her, she arranged to get pregnant, thinking he would have to come back to her then; indeed he wanted to when he heard she was carrying his child. That is why he refused to marry Asha. But his parents and the rest of his family now applied every sort of pressure they could to get Jasvinder to change his mind, and at last they succeeded. He agreed to give up Beth, as she was called, and marry my sister. It was a bad start to a marriage, as you can imagine, and it never worked. They stayed for a while with his family and then went to live in his flat. Asha went into the bedroom and opened the wardrobe. Hanging there was a white wedding dress. In time she knew all about his past life, but it was now too late.

I had been very excited about seeing Asha again after all this time, as we had been very close back in India. But we had changed so much since those days that the old feeling did not return and we were like strangers to each other. I had been a happy laughing little girl then but now I had forgotten how to smile. I had hoped that Asha and my older sisters might take me home with them, at least for a while, but they came only to take me to my own home and left me there, dreading the return of Nirmal.

Of course we had to move again. While I'd been in hospital he had brought girls back to the room and offended the landlord. This time we went to the town hall and applied for a flat as homeless people, and eventually we were given one of our own for the first time. This was a mixed blessing for me, as I depended on kind neighbours to help me; but it was better to have an extra room and our own bathroom and kitchenette. We already had furniture given by Social Security, very old and not very nice to look at, but I was glad of it. For the first time we had white neighbours and I got to know them; it was the first time I had spoken to white people apart from shopkeepers, nurses and social workers. I was lucky as both were very friendly. One was a old lady living alone; she used to talk to me and give me advice and she also gave me my first western clothes. These came from her daughter who was well-off and they were fashionable and pretty. Nirmal wouldn't let me wear them, but I enjoyed trying them on in secret. The other neighbour was middle-aged and living with a married man. Nirmal called her a prostitute and forbade me to talk to her, but she was nice and I did when he was out. She gave me food for the children and taught me how to make jelly. She also gave me an old fridge that had been left in the garden for some time, but it worked in spite of this.

One day as Mrs Roberts, as she was called, was having a cup of tea at my place I left her for a moment to go to the toilet. She, thinking I was in the kitchen, went there too and opened the door which had no lock. She was so surprised by what she saw that instead of closing it at once she just stood and stared, and then she started to laugh. Like the village girl I still was, I was squatting on the toilet seat. We were good friends so I did not feel embarrassed when she told me how to sit down instead.

As a rule, Asian people take very little interest in white people, although they may live amongst them all their lives. The men are usually forced to have some dealings with people from other races, but the women, few of whom work except in Indian shops or factories, often live in a world of their own. Many never learn to speak much English, and this greatly increases their isolation. I know this to my cost. Actually, their life in the Indian community is in some ways the world of the past. Back in India, I am told, there have been many changes in outlook and ways of living and those who go back to visit after several years here often find that life there is freer and more open than it was. I think some people cling to the old ways because they feel insecure. None of my Indian relatives has made white friends. They take advantage of any benefits that they find will help them, but they feel no part of the society they live in.

In India I was told only bad things about the British: that they had taken the wealth from India, which was the 'golden sparrow' they had robbed. They had killed many Indians and put still more in prison for no good reason, and when they left they caused the dreadful fights and massacres that people even a little older than I remembered with horror. I saw a film once which showed how British employers cut off the hands of skilled silk weavers so that they could not work for anyone else. I do not know how true these things are, but my own experience of white people in India was a good one, judging from the hospital my brother Veejay was in for so long, and the hospital that Prem worked in. For some reason I felt drawn to them and used to like watching the way they looked and talked and moved.

When I came to the UK I was told that white people were very immoral and we should not mix with them: that white men and women mix freely, and smoke and drink and go dancing; that husbands leave their wives and children and get divorces. The Indian men I know nearly all drink and smoke, and though they do not usually leave their wives they go after other women if they get the chance. A lot of Indian wives do not expect to enjoy sex, and as far as I know they have little reason to. Husbands do not kiss them on the mouth or court and caress them, even early in marriage; they just make quick use of their bodies for their own satisfaction. I am not saying this only from my own experience, but from talking to many Asian women. The white girls who have Indian boyfriends do expect to enjoy sex, and though some men despise them for this, they also find it very attractive.

Jasvinder, for instance, never gave up Beth; he went to her in secret, and even bought her a flat and paid her an income. She had a little boy and he takes a great interest in the child, more than in his and Asha's two, a boy and girl. Asha knows that the money she earns and has to give to her husband goes partly to support his other family. They have terrible quarrels about it and Asha is sometimes miserable, but nothing ever changes.

16

My life at home went on in much the same way, except it was more difficult with two babies to care for. Koldeep was delicate and had no appetite. I knew I should give both children orange juice and rose-hip syrup, as the health worker had told me, but Nirmal gave me so little money that I could not always get what they needed. I did not know that I could have had free milk and other things as we were living on Social Security. Nirmal smoked heavily and went out drinking as before, but I did not dare to complain. Then, to my horror, Koldeep who was three months old and thin and pale, one day suddenly started to shake all over and jerk his eyes about. I ran out in panic and asked my neighbours to call an ambulance; he was taken to hospital and stayed there for three weeks. He looked much better when he came home, but the same thing happened several times in his first year. Nirmal blamed me for the baby's ill health, but I think it may have been due to malnutrition. It was lucky for me that Hernaik always thrived.

I can't remember now why we moved again, this time to a larger and nicer flat, but in a housing estate, an ugly, bleak and frightening place. None of my neighbours here spoke to me. Here too I came across obvious racial prejudice for the first time; people used to call after me, sometimes in words I could not understand – although I heard them saying 'Blackie' – and the children would throw stones at me. One night Nirmal got into one of his rages and for the first time he threatened me with a knife. I was so frightened I escaped and ran for help. Eventually two policemen arrived and questioned Nirmal and me, and I was able to tell them about the knife and show it too. They took Nirmal away, and this time it was a more serious offence. He appeared in court, and I think he might have been sent to prison, but Anuz and Nimmo persuaded me to ring up and withdraw what I had said, because of the disgrace it would bring on the family, on me and the two children. They also said that the children and I would starve, and I believed this, as I thought it was only Nirmal who could draw Social Security money.

Otherwise I would have been very happy to have him in prison, to feel safe and free. I used to wonder what would happen to me and if I would even live to see my little boys grow up. I could hardly remember that I had once been proud of my pretty looks; I was so thin and wretched-looking and Nirmal told me that I was finished as a woman as I had no bosom. I wondered if I would keep my teeth, as he hit me in the mouth so often, and my front teeth, which were very white and regular, had become loose. Although he did not practice the Sikh religion he wore the steel bracelet, which is a useful weapon. Once when he hit me in the face the bracelet caught my upper lip and split it, so that it bled and bled. I held a cloth to it and hurried to the hospital where it was stitched but it hurt for a long time afterwards. I never told anyone what really happened as Nirmal said he would hurt me much more if I did. There was indeed no escape from Nirmal's cruelty. He made himself a special leather belt with metal studs in it to beat me with, and I was always covered with marks and bruises. My white neighbours here were not so friendly, but I would certainly have gone to them for help, especially as I could now speak a little better, but Nirmal had told me that it was useless for me to do so as he had told them that I was a loose woman, a prostitute, and they would have no pity for me.

Every now and again Nirmal became restless and would take me to stay with his brother's family. Sometimes they were quite glad to have me there to work in the house, and they made me into a drudge. Looking after my two little ones and doing Nimmo's domestic work was too much for me. I was now nineteen and should have been stronger, but I was always tired. It was an effort to get things done and sometimes I had to force myself to take every step. Nimmo constantly found fault with me. The household washing was heavy and she complained that I did it badly. When she told Nirmal, he would beat me and it seemed to me that she enjoyed it. Sometimes Nirmal would leave me and go off somewhere, saying to his brother, 'You made me marry her so now you can keep her.' They certainly did not want me there for good, even as a servant. Anuz would look at me and say, 'I could get a fine girl from India for my brother any time. Her parents would put gold on one side of the scale and the girl on the other, so big would the dowry be. We had to pay two hundred pounds to bring you here. You're no good. We'll send you back and your parents will have to pay us that two hundred pounds.' I believed him and was afraid. My parents would be ruined, the whole family disgraced. I also knew, though, that they would prefer me to die so that they could keep the boys as their own. Boys are valuable. Nimmo would often give me curries to eat that were green with mould. 'Go on, eat,' she would say, 'it's not poison.' But miserable as I was I would not eat and give them the satisfaction of killing me. The day came, however, when they nearly succeeded.

I can't remember why Nirmal started to beat me that day; it went on and on until I was almost out of my mind. I longed to escape even to death. 'I'm going for ever,' I cried, 'I'll kill myself rather than live like this.' Hearing me shout, Nimmo came into the room. I ran to the front door and as I opened it Nirmal shouted, 'All right, do as you please.' I heard Nimmo echo his words as he caught hold of me and threw me outside. As I picked myself up I heard the door being locked behind me. I ran into the street and there I saw Anuz coming towards me as he left the pub on the corner of the street. 'What has happened?' he cried. 'I heard screams coming from our place.'

'Your brother has been battering me, that is why; and now I'm going to kill myself.'

'Go then,' he answered, and slapped my face.

I could think of nothing but escape from pain and hopelessness. Even my children were for that moment forgotten.

The Underground was not far away, so I ran there and started down the stairs. Suddenly I came face to face with a group of women I knew. They were going home from the factory after work. They looked at me in astonishment and crowded around me. 'What are you doing here, running round with your clothes all torn and your feet bare?' I tried to pass them but they held me and started to drag me back. I was by then crying and screaming. If they had not been there and stopped me I know I should have thrown myself in front of the first train, without hesitation and without regret.

The women were shocked and distressed to see me in this state but when they took me back to the flat they dared not say too much as their boss was a friend of Anuz. Anuz and Nimmo and Nirmal may have felt some fear that they would be blamed and looked put out when the women brought me back. They said nothing to me and I went to my room and lay down on the bed exhausted. I cried until I fell asleep for a while. When I woke up I felt numb and unreal. I got up and went into the kitchen. The washing up had been left undone, so I washed the dishes and made some chapatis as if nothing had happened. No one mentioned it again, but the memory of that evening comes back to me time after time.

Meanwhile in India my mother was hearing about what had happened to me as people from our village returned on holiday or came back to stay. Although it is not unusual for girls to be ill-treated when they marry, very few are battered as I was, and you can imagine what misery and guilt my mother felt. She wondered what she could do to help me, but without money she was powerless. Then Asha wrote to her from Leicester asking if she would come over and look after her two little children so that she could go back to work. Asha said she would send over the fare, so Mother made immediate arrangements to come. It was not difficult to get permission. When Asha wrote and told me that Mother was coming I could hardly believe it; I had longed for her so often, and our letters had meant very little. This was because I had never told her the truth about my life.

Mother's fare was paid for to Leicester but she only stayed there for one day. She asked Asha for the fare to London, where she could stay with Indira, and planned to see me as soon as possible. I told Nirmal that she was coming, and as usual he forbade me to go to Indira's place to meet her. I did not care if he killed me as long as I saw Mother! He went out and I put the two children in the old pram and made the long journey to her house. I saw Mother standing at the door looking out for me, and she looked just the same. I had forgotten that I did not, and when she saw me Mother nearly fainted. She leaned against the door and started to cry. I put my arms around her and kept saying, 'I'm all right, Mother.' She hugged me and said that she could hardly recognise me, I was so thin and ill. She was so concerned for me she scarcely noticed the two boys; in fact, as they were Nirmal's children she even felt she could not love them then. We went in and Indira gave us our dinner. I had only seen her occasionally, as Nirmal had quarrelled violently with her husband long ago and he did not welcome me in the house.

Mother and I talked and talked, there was so much to go over. She told me that she was going to take me away, but I did not really think it possible. 'You must think I have a heart of stone', she said, 'to send my poor daughters so far away to take their chance in a strange land, but I did not know. You will not suffer any more.' I told her I must go back home or Nirmal would beat me again and asked her to come with me. Indira wanted her to stay, but Mother said she would go to protect me. 'Who else ever tried to protect you? Nobody,' she said. So we went home, and as Nirmal was late we had time to make plans. Mother told me to go and look for all my documents, my passport, marriage certificate, and the children's birth certificates. I went through Nirmal's papers and found them. Then she told me to pack a few things for myself and the children, but to say nothing to him. He came back very late and Mother had gone into the bedroom to rest. She heard him shout and abuse me and I thought she might come in and protect me, but when she did she was very polite to Nirmal, even flattering, and I realised that she was a clever woman. He started to confide in her, telling her that he was short of money and had bills he could not pay. She was sympathetic and said, 'I will take Sita and the children back to

Leicester with me for a few days. We will stay with Asha and you will be able to save some money for your bills. I will pay the fares for them.' Nirmal was pleased to think he would have us out of the way for a while and a bit more money to drink and gamble with. He agreed and even went to bed in a better temper than usual. He thought my mother approved of him!

Next morning I got ready to go, terrified that Nirmal would find I had taken the papers. He came with us to the station, but irritable as he often was in the morning he found fault with me. 'What do you think you look like, stupid thing, in those dreadful old clothes? You should be ashamed.' He began to kick me in front of everyone on the platform. Still my mother said nothing, though she told me afterwards that her hands were clenched so hard that they pained her. We got into the train and Nirmal stood outside by the half-open window. Just before the train started, Mother came to the window and spoke to him in a loud clear voice. 'You will never see even the shadow of my daughter again.' I thought with terror that he would jump on the train and pull me out on to the platform, but he stood there without moving, too astonished to do anything. The train started, he turned away and I hoped I would be free of him for ever. My wonderful mother had saved my life. Now a new life would begin for me and my children.

17

As the train gathered speed and left London behind I felt excited and hopeful. I looked out of the window and saw green fields with sheep and cows, and trees and distant hills and rivers. Although it was winter still it seemed beautiful to me after being shut indoors for so long. I had been on a train before, when we went to Delhi and Amritsar, but this was even better. I still feel that to go on a train is a great adventure. After a while, when the first excitement had died down, I had time to think about what had happened. Surely this was too good to be true? It was almost impossible for an Indian woman to escape from her husband. He would follow me, beat me, and drag me back. I said this to Mother. 'Don't worry,' she said. 'Leicester is far away and you will be safe with Asha and me and her family.'

'Does Asha know that I am coming to her, and more, that I am never going back?'

'No', said Mother. 'Let them think that you are just coming for a holiday. I will tell them gradually.'

I knew that Mother was both brave and clever. How else could she have travelled alone from Leicester to London and found Indira's house, with hardly a word of English and knowing nothing of English ways? How cunning she was in getting us away so easily, with all the documents, and how brave in standing up to Nirmal and defying him at the last moment on the train. It takes courage to go against the customs of our people. I realised I must have faith in Mother and build up my own courage. After all, I was now twenty years old and the mother of two sons. True, I knew very little and had had no chance to learn about life over here, but now

I had my opportunity and must take it. I looked at my two little boys; Hernaik was strong and lively, but Koldeep was very small for his age and had been delicate from birth, probably because I had been beaten and half-starved while I was carrying him. Now both my sons would be happier and healthier without their father. Mother went on reassuring me and I was able to relax and fall asleep. I was so tired I slept and slept the whole journey, and she cared for the children and watched over me.

Asha and her husband Jasvinder, who had a business and was doing quite well, and their two children, lived in a flat in a tall dark house. There was not much room, but they welcomed us kindly and gave us a good meal. Because I had not wanted Nirmal to suspect anything I had not packed many clothes; not even nappies for Koldeep as they had not been dry, so Asha had to provide us with extra things. I had thought them very heartless for not helping me in London when everyone knew how dreadfully I was being treated, and I am still puzzled by this, for I know I would have saved a younger sister if I had been well off and used to this country. However, I must say that at this time and until I became more independent they were of great help to me. Possibly this was due to the influence of my mother.

Next day they both went off to work and Mother and I looked after their two children and mine. Mother did the cooking, Indian style, but we also ate things new to me, like porridge and cheese, and bread and butter. As the days went by, Mother gradually told Asha more about my life with Nirmal. I did not know at the time that she believed that I was going to die. It was not only that I was so thin, but she said I had a shrivelled look that she had seen on people in India who were dying. No wonder she cried when she first saw me! She told Asha this, and others who came to the house, and they were sorry for me. Eventually after a week or so she confessed to Asha that I had left Nirmal and would never go back. She and her husband understood and they did not blame me.

I knew that we would hear from Nirmal when we did not return and that he would never believe that Mother meant what she said. Sure enough, he phoned when the week was up and I had to speak to him. The phone in my hand shook so much I thought I would drop it, and my voice would not come. At last I managed to say, 'No I'm not coming' and put the phone down. Then I felt sick and ill all day. He phoned again two days later, and again I said no and felt sick and ill with fear. This time he was angry and started to shout, saying that he would come here and kill me. Next day I was terrified that he would appear at the door and seize hold of me. Mother and I talked it over and decided that I must leave Asha's and find a place of my own where I would be safer.

There were many Asians living in our street so it was not hard to find a room. It was in a horrible house and the room was dark and smelly. It had a bed, a table and little more, but it was very cheap. I would have to share kitchen and bathroom with several others. I brought the children here and had now to look after them myself. I still felt weak and always very tired, so I could not enjoy the children and play with them, but Hernaik seemed happy and Koldeep was getting stronger. Asha's husband told me to go to Social Security, so I went with Asha and she explained things to them for me. I was given fourteen pounds a week, which was not much, even then, but they wanted to be sure that I was telling the truth and not just staying for a holiday. After three months I was given the full amount, but meanwhile Asha helped me, and some of the Indian ladies who lived nearby gave me food and clothes.

I felt a little safer in my new place, but there were still dangers to be faced apart from Nirmal coming after me. Mother had always visited the temple at home, so she started to attend the one nearest to us. I went too, but we soon found that the people there were against us. Everyone blamed Mother for taking me away from my husband, saying that I would be on my own when she died with no one to look after me, and what would become of me then? For them a woman on her own is unthinkable; she has no status, and if she is young it is taken for granted that she will be immoral. They hinted that I would probably become a prostitute. Instead of feeling happy and at peace when I went to the temple, I felt very depressed and out of place. Mother was a fighter and defied them all. She did not believe that it is better for a woman to stay with her husband even if it killed her, and she felt sure that she would live long enough to see me safe and independent. Nevertheless, she stayed within the community and did not feel herself a stranger there as I was beginning to do. Because of this attitude among the temple people we were afraid that pressure would be put on me to return to my husband.

The leaders of our community are the priests and the wealthy and important people who attend the temple and look after its affairs. They are of course all men. They do sometimes try to solve marriage problems, and Mother and I were afraid that Nirmal would go to them in London and ask them to send someone to Leicester to talk to the local leaders here. They might well believe Nirmal, who would tell them lies, and I would get the blame and be shamed into returning to him. As we heard later he did try this, but fortunately his reputation was too bad for them to offer to help him.

Just at this time when I was feeling so weak and sad, a good thing happened. Our guru, the Baba Charon Singh, was coming to London and would receive new members into his sect, the Rahda Swami. It would be possible for me to go as there would be free coach travel to and from London for his followers. Mother and Asha and my sister from Leeds all wanted to go as well. We had never seen the guru, and this was a great privilege. I knew what he looked like because Asha had several big photographs of him on the walls of her flat, and Mother had one of her own in a frame. He is old and looks very wise and calm. He had a long white beard and is dressed in white.

The coach was full, not only with Indians but with many white people too. Our guru has millions of followers in India, but in other countries all over the world there are many who believe in him and follow him. He does not despise other religions but accepts them, whether they are Sikh, Hindu, Buddhist, Christian or Moslem, and quotes from their holy men. His is a religion for everyone and anyone who is prepared to obey him.

When we arrived in London we were taken to a very big hall. It was completely full, but we could see the guru clearly as he was sitting on a stage under a canopy. Another man read from a holy book and the guru explained what it meant. Everyone was very quiet. Later we went upstairs to a big room where about two hundred people were waiting to be received. Some hoped to be selected, others were admirers who wanted a chance to see the guru face to face. We waited in a line as he spoke to each of us in turn. He asked each one the same question, 'Have you abstained from animal foods, alcohol and tobacco for at least three months?' Those who answered no were told to go by a gesture of the guru's hand. Helpers were standing by; they quietly took these people by the arm and led them away in case they wanted to stay and talk. Sometimes the guru just looked into a person's face and knew that they were not suitable. He did not speak, just moved his hand to dismiss them. These people were very upset. When it came to my turn I found that I was crying; I felt the guru knew and understood my sadness and troubles. I could answer truthfully that I had not done any of the forbidden things; he looked into my face and allowed me to pass on.

Those of us who were selected, about one hundred and fifty I think, gathered in another room, where the guru was sitting in view. He started to tell us how we must live from now on, abstaining from the forbidden things and living simply, without desires. It is wanting things that makes us unhappy, but without wants we can be happy and at peace. To do this we must meditate every day for two and a half hours, and we will be given a holy name which is never to be spoken aloud, only remembered in prayer. He called this holy name out, the same for all those selected. We had now to be true to the guru and to the holy name for ever. Members of the sect then came round to each of us and helped us to remember the five words of the holy name.

Next we were told how to meditate. We must see a picture of the guru in our minds, just as he is, sitting, moving and talking, and keep it there all the time. Our minds will be lifted up by the guru until we are close to God. After a while we will hear the guru talking to us, but first we must learn not to listen to our minds talking about all the ordinary things in life. There are dangers too in meditating that we must avoid, for there are demons that will try to get into your mind and destroy the picture of the guru. They may even make themselves look just like the guru and say wrong things to make you lose the path, but you must look into their eyes to find them out. Their eyes always give them away.

Whatever happens to you is your karma, brought with you from a previous life, and if you have pain and sorrow that is why. If you lead a good life and keep the image of the guru always before you, he will be responsible for you always, and when you die he will be there to take you to God and to judgement. The guru knows all about you, where you are and everything you do. If you follow him your life will be peaceful, happy and fortunate, for you are under his protection. Some of this I knew already, but I had never taken it too seriously. Now I had been selected and given the holy name I began to feel worried. I knew I could never meditate like that, my mind was always full of all kinds of little things that would not go away. I could not accept the karma of being with Nirmal. If I had done so, what would have become of my children? I think I would have died soon and left them to him. Besides, I did not want to feel guilty if I wanted a new dress or something for the house, or if I went out with friends. I did not tell anyone, but my feelings were very mixed. I was frightened, too, because the guru would know already what I was thinking, and if I gave him up after being selected it would be a great sin and I would be very unlucky. To this day I have never been a wholehearted follower as my mother was and my sisters still are. I believe the guru is right in many ways, and I certainly will never eat animal foods. I try to lead a good life and remember to pray to God for help, but I feel I must make my own way for myself and my children.

When I was back at home I tried to learn more by reading the holy books. I have one in our language, but it is difficult for me to understand as it is in poetry, and more difficult to translate into English for my friend. It says that the guru is just like a man on earth, and most people do not recognise that he is really a god. Although he lives in the world his soul is in heaven and he comes here to help us to get to know God. He is very close to Him, and through the guru we can get close too. Sometimes he performs miracles. When I was in London, I heard of one. Some thieves were trying to break down the door of a house belonging to an Indian family who were followers of his. They were not at home at the time, but an English lady who lived next door looked out to see what was happening. She saw an old man in white open the door and tell the thieves to go away, which they did. When the family returned this lady visited them to tell them what had happened. 'Can you describe the old man?' they asked. She looked round and said, 'Yes, that's him', and pointed to a big photo of the guru. I was astonished when my sister in Leeds told me that once the guru appeared in her house and sat down to a meal with her. I am not sure that I believe this.

18

Now at this time an Indian woman who had divorced her husband lived in a town nearby. One night her ex-husband came to her door, forced his way in and killed her by stabbing her five times with his knife. Everyone was talking about it. The man was caught and tried and is in prison to this day. You can imagine how frightened I was when I heard about it. I was afraid to be alone in the house and afraid to go out as well. A few weeks went by and nothing further happened, but just as I was beginning to feel more confident Nirmal suddenly appeared and called on Asha. She refused to let him in and told him she did not know where I had gone. He said he would find me and kill me. After he'd gone she ran round to warn me. I was terrified. She told me we must go to the police, so as soon as it was dark we crept out, very scared lest he might be hiding near, and went to the police station. Asha told them how Nirmal had come to her house and threatened to find me and kill me. A policeman asked to see my passport, took notes and said they would look out for him. If he came to me I should let them know. I did not feel much safer because of this as it might well be too late by the time they police arrived!

Meanwhile, I heard later, Nirmal had been to see my Uncle Deen who also lived with his family in Leicester. He was only a distant relative and although Mother and I had visited him he had not offered to help in any way. Because he was wealthy he thought his family very superior to ours and did not want to be involved. However, he did agree to help Nirmal and went with him to Asha's. They stood at the door because again she would not let Nirmal in. Mother came up behind her and when she saw Nirmwal her anger came out. She shouted at him that he had starved and beaten me. 'She is nothing but a bag of bones,' she cried, 'and you will never have the chance to ill-treat her again.' The two men were silenced and went away. We had a family conference and it was decided that it was too dangerous for me to be on my own, even so near to them. Jasvinder said I would be safer living in their house. There was a little flat on the floor above them that he could buy for only seventeen hundred pounds. It would be an investment and I could live there and pay him rent, which I would receive from Social Security. It had two rooms and a kitchen and bathroom, so it would be much better for me. They also gave me some old furniture and cooking utensils and we soon moved in. I was very pleased, for it was the only time I had had a kitchen all to myself, without even Nirmal to spoil it.

Although I had been in Leicester for several weeks I had not improved much in health. Perhaps it was all the strain and fear on top of the misery I had endured in London that held me back. I had little appetite, was still as thin as a bone, and was always trembling. My periods had stopped now for two years, and my breasts had shrivelled like an old woman's. I suppose it was fortunate in a way as otherwise I might have had another child or even two, and I doubt if I would have survived that. Asha said I should see a doctor and I agreed, but not an Asian one. A local doctor took me on his list and I found he was kind and patient, listening to my story. I remember he looked at my neck and into my eyes and then asked me to rest a book on my outstretched arms. The book shook very much. After several other tests he told me that I must take certain tablets and attend a hospital. I was quite happy to do this as I liked hospitals and had usually been treated very well. I still thought that one day perhaps I would be a nurse. I was given injections for many months and began to feel better fairly soon.

Mother and I were now together most of our time and we became closer than we had ever been. She still felt very protective towards me. Now Nirmal was far away she could get fond of the children who were indeed very lovable and attractive. Hernaik was very like me, with my big dark eyes and rather regular features. Koldeep was more like his father, but unlike him his eyes were sparkling and he had a lovely smile. A social worker came to see us and she was kind and helpful. I learned from her that Nirmal had been to Social Security in London and told the people there many lies. One reason why he was so angry at my going away was that he was so much poorer without any allowance for a wife and two children and no child benefit. He had kept most of this himself before, for drink, gambling and cigarettes. He told them that he had sent me away on holiday and had given me a hundred pounds to spend, that he had always treated me well and now he wanted me to return. He hoped that after this I would receive no more money and be forced to return. Fortunately, he was not believed and I was, so his plan failed. I felt really pleased to think of him trying to manage on a single man's allowance. This social worker also told us about classes in English, so Mother and I went to one quite near and enjoyed it. Mother did not learn very well, perhaps she was too old, but I began to understand much better and have more confidence in talking.

Several months went by and it seemed that Nirmal had forgotten us, but we were wrong. He phoned Asha and told her that he was coming up to Leicester. The anxiety started all over again for me and Mother, and we felt weak and ill with strain. Soon after this some of the community leaders came to see us and told us that Nirmal had applied to them for help in restoring his family. They did not know as much about him as they had in London. They said that they knew he had behaved badly in the past and that he had admitted it, but now he was sorry and promised to make a fresh start. As I was living in the same house as my mother and sister, Nirmal could not harm me without their knowing. Also they, the community leaders, would be watching us to ensure that the children and I were safe. I suppose I felt too weak to go on fighting. These men were old and wise and must be respected. Everyone but Mother put pressure on me to give in. Mother never believed that Nirmal had changed, and she was suspicious of him particularly since he had insisted that if he returned to live here the members of my family must keep

away and not enter his house. Because I knew I could visit
them instead, I was not as put off by this as I should have
been. It was certainly not for any love of me that he wanted to
start again. I knew he had not even been faithful to me while
I was with him, but he may have had some need for the
children. It is true he had never considered their health and
happiness in London, but perhaps most of all, even more
than the money, it was pride. He could not face the shame of
being left by his wife and deprived of his sons. I wondered
if he also needed me as someone to punish when he was in a
bad mood, for he had no one else to torment now. I tried to
look on the bright side, and believe that Nirmal had realised
he would have to treat me well or lose me. Everyone but
Mother would blame me if I did not take him back. Maybe
he would respect me more since I had shown independence,
and at least he would not dare to attack me again. I agreed to
have him back.

It was arranged that Nirmal should return to live with me
in a few days' time. I felt very tense and anxious in spite of
my good resolutions. He was expected during the day, but
when he had not arrived at seven at night I put the boys to
bed. Half an hour later I heard very loud music on the stair
and guessed it was him. He came in with a cassette player in
his hand, and it seemed like an act of defiance. Hardly greet-
ing me, he asked to see the children and went into the
bedroom. On his return, he looked around the room and
said, 'This furniture is no good. You must throw out those
chairs tomorrow. And the bed next door: that must go too.
Your brother-in-law charges rent. He must give me proper
furniture.' I said nothing as I saw he had been drinking
before he came. I could smell it on his breath. When he came
near me I shrank away disgusted and he laughed and said,
'Don't be afraid. I won't even touch you. I would trust no
woman who had been on her own so long. How do I know if
another man has had you or not?' It was useless for me to
deny this, and in a way it was a relief, in spite of the insult, as
I certainly did not want him to touch me.

Asha had a friend who was a nurse and she had taken me
to Family Planning. She advised me to have injections to

prevent pregnancy as she thought I might find it difficult to manage my own contraception. Later we heard that these injections can be dangerous but I was glad to be free from worry, as to have another child then would have been dreadful: I had resolved to refuse to have sex with Nirmal but I knew he might insist and force me.

Nirmal now opened his suitcase and took out a number of nice new blouses. He put them in a plastic bag and said, 'You can keep my dinner for me, I'm going to the pub.' I knew that during his visits he had made friends with people in the local pub and later heard that he had given the blouses to the barmaids and other women there, showing them the cards from this factory where he was now working and pretending he was a wealthy man from London. At about eleven-thirty he retuned home drunk and when I went into the kitchen to heat his food he followed me in and started to shout at me and swear, just as before. He punched me and pulled my hair so hard that a piece was torn away from my scalp. I screamed with pain and fear, but he said that if I screamed again he would throw me out of the window. To show he meant it he ran across and opened the window.

Now Mother had been worried when she knew Nirmal was coming, but she did not appear as she knew she must keep away. She crept down and waited outside my door. When Nirmal went out and did not return for hours she went downstairs and stayed with a neighbour, thinking she might be able to hear better. However, she fell asleep and heard nothing. Nirmal took his food and continued to drink beer that he had brought back in cans. He told me I must get up early next morning and go with him to Social Security and tell them that I no longer needed the money as my husband was back. He would get the money for all of us. As he got drunker, he told me of his plan. He would convince my family and the community leaders that he was being good to me, and if I dared to complain he would beat me. Then he would take me and the children to London and make my life so miserable there that I would be glad to leave and let him have his sons. 'After that I don't care what happens to you,' he said.

I was wondering how I could escape. At some time he was sure to go to the toilet, so I waited quietly. As soon as he went stumbling out I rushed to the door and up the stairs. I beat on Asha's door, shouting and crying. She and Jasvinder were in bed but came quickly to let me in. Jasvinder phoned the police and very soon two men arrived. This time I was able to tell them what had happened. They asked me if I had a rent book and fortunately I had it there. I was told that Nirmal could not stay in my flat against my will. I heard them go down stairs and talk to Nirmal, and I heard him saying, 'Go away, it's none of your business. I won't go with you.' Of course they took him away, and I cried with relief.

Nirmal was taken to the police station and kept in a cell, as they had searched him and found he had a knife. Next day he was allowed to go as long as he returned to London. He came round to my place to collect his things, but I wouldn't open the door. 'You can have them if you return with a policeman,' I told him. He did, so I let him in. I had already opened his suitcase and found he had brought back many of my saris so I took them out and hid them. As he was packing his stuff he demanded the saris but I took no notice. The policeman did not understand our language of course so Nirmal swore at me and threatened me all the time until he went. At last I was free, but for how long? It seemed to me that he was a curse put upon my life, and I had no escape.

19

In spite of all the bad things that had happened to me there was something in me that blindly and, almost without my knowing, went on hoping and struggling for life. I vowed I would not let Nirmal destroy me and my children. I would never again let the temple people persuade me to give in, nor would gossiping neighbours be able to make me feel ashamed and outcast. I went about the city and looked at the shops. Some of them were big and beautiful and I loved the fashionable dresses in the windows. I can still spend hours window shopping. Spring was coming and I took the boys to the park to enjoy the first warm sunshine. I like the cool weather here after the heat of India. There were many people walking in the parks and I would see men and women to-gether, hand-in-hand, talking, laughing and even kissing. I had never seen this before. I found myself giving deep sighs as I watched them. What could it be like to have a kind and loving man? I did not hate men because of Nirmal. I felt a warm light inside me that longed for love, and the faith that I would have this love from a man some day helped to keep me from despair.

Asha advised me to get a divorce, so after talking to the social worker we went to see a lawyer. She explained that I must wait for two years' separation before this was possible, but it would cost nothing as I was entitled to legal aid. It was lucky for me that Asha was more educated than my other three sisters for when they heard that I would be getting a divorce they wrote and sent messages blaming me for ruining the marriage chances of all their daughters. Who would want to marry the nieces of a divorced woman? It was impossible for them to imagine anything but an arranged marriage and a dowry for these girls, but Asha and her husband thought that little Kanta should have a good education, a job if she wished, and a choice of suitable husbands, preferably a love match to someone of her own kind. I certainly thought this a very good idea, but my other sisters would never accept it, and I did feel guilty for worrying them so.

We did not know how Nirmal would react to the divorce, and in case he got difficult and came here again to seek me out we decided that I should move again, this time to somewhere far from our part of the city. I explained this to the social worker and asked her if she could help me to find a suitable place. That was how I came to live here on a housing estate a few miles from the city centre. She took me to see a flat in a smallish block, not too high, and I was very pleased with it as it was clean and modern, had a lounge and two bedrooms, kitchen and bathroom very much nicer than I had ever had before. It was very much better than Asha's own flat too, and I wondered why she and her husband were content to live in such a shabby, cramped place, with miserable furniture and no comfort. Many Indians live this way, saving money for trips to India or investing in property at home, helping their relatives back in the villages, or for starting their own businesses here. Jasvinder, of course, had another family to keep, a very sore point with Asha naturally enough.

My new flat was very nice, but of course I had no furniture or household goods, apart from the few that had been given to me. Here again Social Security came to my aid and provided me with all the essentials of life. The furniture was not new or smart but it gave me a very good start. Moving in was quite exciting and I was pleased to be on my own, except that I missed Mother; I wished she could live with me, but she had come here to help Asha with the children and they gave her a home in return. Once I moved in, however, I did see Mother every day. In the mornings and early afternoons she was at home with the children; when Asha came home at four she went to work in a clothing factory for four hours, then got a bus and made the long journey to the estate. She spent the evening with me, lest I should be lonely, and then stayed the night so that I would be safe. She had to be up early so as to be in time for Asha to go to work. Poor mother – she had worked so hard all her life, and now she was quite old there was no rest for her. I think she was so used to being always busy that she had never learned to relax, even if it had been possible for her. Now she was driven by her desire to help me and Indira and to be independent as she had always been – strong, standing on her own and proud.

20

Although I did not realise it at the time, the move was a very important step in my life because I was for the first time on my own among white people who knew nothing about me and who would accept me without criticism because I had left my husband. I had to speak English all the time and think for myself as Indian women seldom do because they lack confidence in their own judgements; they often go round asking for advice from all their family and friends, which only adds to their problems because they get confused by so many different opinions. One of the first things I did was to visit my new neighbours, so I knocked on the nearest door and met Margaret, a friendly girl who asked me to tea next day and gave me toast and golden syrup. After this she often came to my house, and she also introduced me to her mother-in-law who lived near us. I was always welcome to drop in on her, and I would help her with her housework. In return she would look after my boys if I wanted to go out shopping. Another neighbour was Susan who gave me trousers and tee-shirts, the first western clothes I dared to wear outside. I never came across any racial prejudice on the estate, perhaps because I experienced none myself. I was very ready to like white people and did not find them to be the way many Indians say they are. My mother also got on very well with them too. When she got off the bus at night if there were any teenagers there they would carry her bags and walk her home.

Just as I was beginning to be happy here a new disaster struck me. It was only now that I discovered my passport had run out, and when I tried to get it renewed I learned I had been an illegal immigrant for nearly all this time. My visa had been for three months, until I married in fact, and Nirmal should have sent my passport in with evidence of marriage. He had neglected to do this either deliberately or through carelessness. We were so overwhelmed by this that in despair I thought I would have to go back to the village to a hopeless life, with no chance of escape from my reputation as a divorced and disgraced wife, no means of earning a living, and with a slur on my children as well as on myself. I felt bitter that in our culture men are never to blame; Nirmal could be accepted in spite of his dreadful faults; he could marry again and go on as before and get away with it. I who had done no harm and suffered so much must be the outcast. I felt at this time like someone battered by stones. I would struggle to my feet to escape, but another stone would hit me and I would fall again. I wondered sometimes if God was punishing me, or was it because I had sinned in a previous life? Mother used to wonder too and would look at me sadly and say, 'Why are other girls so much luckier than you?' I could not hurt her by saying that nearly all of us in the family were unlucky, the girls mostly because of bad husbands. I could not say either that most of this ill-luck came from having a father who was irresponsible and foolish and left too many burdens for my mother to bear and too many difficult decisions for her to take.

You may have noticed that in my life I have lucky chances as well as bad ones. Often a good person comes into my life and helps me when I need help most. In the social work department a girl called Felicity took great trouble over my case. She wrote letters and phoned and went on and on until the whole matter of my passport was cleared up. She advised me to apply for British citizenship to safeguard my future, so I did. I was alarmed when I learned that it would cost me two hundred pounds, although it would have been only seventy pounds if my marriage had been known at the time.

Now it happened that soon after this I was lucky again. One day in town I recognised someone I had known at home. It was Vilma the Harajan girl. She did not know me, because in spite of being better in health I was still very thin and pale, but when I greeted her she was very pleased to see me. As I said before, she was now married and quite well-off, with three children. I went back with her to see her flat and all her furniture and clothes, which she showed me proudly. They had big colour TV and a video. While the children were at school and her husband at work, Vilma would spend all day looking at Indian films, dressing her hair, manicuring her nails, putting on make-up, and so on. She had plenty of jewellery and many expensive saris. Vilma was bored and lonely and I said I would visit her often in return and we would see films together. When I told her of my difficulties she said she would lend me the money when I needed it and I could pay it back in my own time, and indeed, she did. It would be very hard for me to pay back such a large sum, but that was in the future and who could know what would happen. Mother used to say, 'Always believe you will succeed' and also 'Watch to see which way the oil is flowing'.

I continued to explore the way of life on the estate. I was delighted to find that the girlfriends I made treated me just like one of them. Although not yet twenty-one, by Indians I was considered finished as a woman; my new friends thought my life had hardly begun. They took it for granted that I should enjoy life, have pretty clothes, and go about freely. They asked me if I had any boyfriends and were surprised that I had not. I went to the shops with Susan and she showed me the fashionable ones, not just the cheapest chain stores I had tried before. I began to buy western clothes, though it was usually at jumble sales, and my friends advised me what to wear. Although I know that to look really beautiful a woman cannot do better than wear a sari, especially one made of silk in delicate or rich colours and with fine embroidery, to me Indian clothes had become associated with a sad and narrow restricted life, and these new clothes represented freedom. Mother was worried at first, so I had to be careful not to go too far. She became used to seeing me in trousers, but a skirt, never. It is considered that only a loose woman will show her legs. Most Indian women use make-up when they are married, and I wanted to too, but Mother thought it unsuitable for me in my position. Although she was so bold in fighting for my rights she was still in the community and always would be, and she wanted me to be beyond criticism. One thing she did agree to and that was to go with me to the films, where we went every week. This was partly because as an elderly person she was given free tickets for Indian films. There were several film houses specially for these films, before videos were so common. They were not considered suitable for unmarried women, as they were said to be sexy, but they were much more romantic than erotic, and the film stars were never even seen to kiss. This was another example of mother going against the community for me, because she knew how much I enjoyed them.

My two boys were now going to nursery school, speaking English and making friends. I could not tell and still do not know if Hernaik in particular has been affected by all the violence, threats and shouting that he experienced while we were with Nirmal. Physically they have not suffered I believe, even Koldeep, as both boys have fine, strong, straight limbs and good clear complexions. They are very lively and quick-witted, and seem very confident. I think they have done well partly because I have given them a varied and part western diet, even meat and fish and eggs, and they greatly prefer these foods to curries. In India the food we ate was usually good. The flour was stone-ground, vegetables and fruit very fresh and as a rule the women took a great interest in tasty and varied cooking. In Britain they still eat curries most of the time, but they eat white bread and rice, very few vegetables unless frozen or canned, little fruit and a lot of sugar and sweets. I cannot help noticing that my boys look stronger and better-built than many other children of Indian parents from villages like ours. I had not done so well, as the doctor had told me when I first went to see him in Leicester that I had rickets due to malnutrition, and I had to take capsules of oil for this.

I too enjoyed some western foods, but I have always kept to my vegetarian diet. I did not smoke or drink as many of my new friends did, but I did one bold thing after a great deal of thought; I went to the hairdresser and had my long plait cut off. The style I chose was shoulder-length and with my thick black shiny hair I thought it really looked good. I dreaded Mother seeing it for the first time, and she was very shocked, but I have never regretted it. Those single schoolgirl plaits are very unattractive and look absurd on older women. Mother's attitude was a strange one. She said, 'You should think of your position. It is not as if you are anyone special, without even a job.' I was hurt by this, that Mother should think so little of me, but I suppose it was really that she did not want me to look attractive and draw attention to myself in case I should not appear respectable, and the community could say 'We told you she would become an immoral woman.' When Asha saw my hair she went and had hers cut the same way, but this was all right as she was not only a married woman but a businesswoman too.

I found out that some of the girls on the estate really were immoral when they persuaded me to go to a disco where there were bars serving beer and wine and so on. I wore my sari and the men there were respectful, but I discovered that one or two of the girls would spend the night with a man even if they did not know him well. They called this a 'one-night stand'. These girls were single parents; some had been divorced, others had illegitimate children. This surprised me as they were pleasant, friendly girls. I was also taken to a Singles Club, where separated and divorced people could meet to find new partners. These men and women were usually older and seemed coarse and noisy. Many of the women were overdressed and wore heavy make-up, and the men often drank too much. I disliked this club with its smell of drink and tobacco smoke. This was one place where I saw the seamy side of British society. I preferred the group I went to of about eight single mothers who met to discuss our problems, and the family centre where mothers often took their children and had tea or coffee together. Certainly I was never lonely and was surprised to find how easy it was to make friends. No day went by without my having someone to talk to or go out with.

I had never realised how many women there were, like me, living on their own without a man, and often with children, some illegitimate. It was an unnatural life and it made many of them desperate for change and excitement as they found things dull at home. This drove them to the clubs and bars and discos to meet men. Like me, too, they were often living on welfare payments and had little money to spend, and they hoped the men would pay for drinks and entertainments. Of course many of the girls hoped too that they would find a man to love and marry them, but it seemed to me that the men were looking just for sex. This made the girls become hard and cynical, especially the older ones, but mostly they were still good mothers, and I found them kind friends. I could never be like them; my culture, my own nature, and the shocks I had had in marriage prevented me. But they accepted me as I was and respected me.

One of my neighbours was Sally, a very pretty girl who had two children by different men. She had been let down by both of them, but she was not downhearted, just determined to escape from a rather dreary life. By pretending to have a job and getting friends to sign forms for her, she bought new furniture and a big TV and many other things on the never-never. For a whole year she hardly paid any rent for her council flat. She used to get a newspaper sent to her that had adverts in it for people wanting partners, and Sally spent a lot of time writing letters to men. She went to London, all expenses paid, and stayed a week. Later on another man invited her for Christmas and gave her a hundred pounds to spend. When she came back she was very cheerful. One evening she came to see me and told me she was flitting in the small hours next morning. This 'bloke', she said, had asked her to marry him, and she was going to London, 'kids and all'. She was leaving all her debts behind, and asked me if I would like to take her TV or any of the other things she had on the HP. 'No one will know that you have them,' she said, 'so don't miss the chance.' I said no, as I did not want to be involved. I never saw Sally again, and I have often wondered if she was successful in her new life. Although I could not do such things and know that they are wrong, I could not, having had a friendship from girls like Sally, feel like blaming them too much. I had seen far worse things being done.

21

Although I did not want to blame or criticise people too much, the Asian community was very busy criticising me. From the first they had thought it strange that I should want to live apart from my own people, among white strangers. It is all very well, they think, for the wealthy and well educated to mix with British people, but not for a poor and simple girl like me, without a husband or even a job. It is very hard indeed to go against the community, and I think I could do it only because of two things: one was the unusual cruelty I had suffered with Nirmal, the other the feeling I had always had that there was something different about me. I could not describe it, and I did not understand it, but it was there. Mother only understood that it was necessary for me to be safe, far away from where Nirmal would find me, and she stood up for me; but it was hard for her to be always fighting on my behalf and, after being so respected, to be criticised herself. The gossips said that I was going astray, even sooner than expected. Why else should I wear western clothes and cut my hair? Men would say that I was every night in the pubs drinking and flirting with white men; smoking and dancing too. In fact, of course, I was at home most of the time with my boys, or with my girlfriends. A free woman is a threat to the Asian community, and they only feel safe if girls and women are kept in their place as wives and mothers in the very narrow world of the average Indian woman. I realised during my life on the estate that there are dangers in freedom, but they did not affect me. I did not want freedom to be promiscuous, but to find myself and be independent. I would never have developed without striking out for myself; the five years of marriage had wounded me too deeply.

I cannot say that I was really free of Nirmal, because I could not forget him. He would come into my dreams and I would cry out in fear. When I woke up I was nervous and depressed and sometimes felt, in spite of all my efforts, that he had won. Something in my mind had been beaten down and was still hurt and broken, but I would think of my children and Mother and the freedom of my new life, and the glow of light inside me would burn up again and heal me. At Christmas Nirmal phoned Asha, but all through that year he never came to seek us out.

I started my second year on the estate without much change. Sometimes I quarrelled with Mother and wished she was not always there watching me and warning me and telling me what people were saying, and we would part on bad terms. After she had gone I would remember how I loved her and how much I owed her and would phone up to say I was sorry. Even Asha was less friendly these days, although we still visited each other and the children played together. After all, I had gone much further in taking freedom than she had, in spite of her education, her good English and her work in business. Perhaps she was jealous of me, and I must admit I was jealous of her in some ways, of her fine clothes, their car, and the holidays they could take with their children. Jasvinder, too, had become suspicious of me, perhaps believing the bad things said, but we did not quarrel until one day when I was at their house and Asha and he had an argument. It was nothing very serious, about her spending money, for Asha had to ask him for every penny, but he had been drinking and got into a rage. He started to shout and abuse her, and then to hit her in the face. Then I got angry and shouted to him to stop being such a brute. Of course he turned on me then and pushed me out of the door, telling me never to come back. The bitterness that came from this did not die down, in fact it grew, and for some time I avoided going to Asha's house while he was there. Many Indian women I know over here take it for granted that their husbands will beat them sometimes; as long as it is not too serious they accept it. I myself could never accept it again and could never marry an Indian man unless I was sure he had different values. After this quarrel, Asha could not help me much as her husband forbade it and she had to do it in secret. She was always complaining about him, but has never had the courage to leave him.

I continued to make friends on the estate. One married couple with children invited me and the boys to spend Christmas with them. We thought this was wonderful. I joined a Keep-Fit class on the estate and enjoyed it. It was there I had my first experience of love since those days long ago when, as a young girl, I had loved Rama. The instructor was a handsome young man with a fine figure, and I felt the first stirrings of interest that reminded me that I was still a woman. I used to find excuses to talk to him, to stay behind with a question, or stop in the street for a chat. I felt excited and nervous, and my eyes were shining like stars when I went home thinking about him. Nothing came of it; he was friendly and kind, but I could see that he was indifferent to me as a woman. My hopes died down and my heart cooled, but I was glad I had felt this way; it made me feel more real, like other girls.

Another year passed, quite a happy one, without much further change, apart from the boys growing up and starting school. It was strange to have such big children while I was so young. My real age was twenty-two, but on my passport it was twenty-eight, and I dared not change it for fear of trouble. It must have been a puzzle to doctors and social workers that I looked so young. Although my life now was fairly secure I never believed my luck would last, and indeed a new series of misfortunes started. I began to feel very tired and weak, so much so that I went to my doctor and told him. He sent me to hospital for tests and I was told that I must stay in for several weeks. There was a home for children just nearby; the boys could still attend school and I would be able to see them. I was glad to know that I could be treated, but when I told mother she was very disturbed. She thought it dreadful that the children should be away from home, and she was terrified of doctors and hospitals. Fortunately she had always been healthy and only needed to dose herself with traditional Indian herbs and spices. She thought I should do the same. 'There is nothing wrong with you,' she said, 'you just need a rest.'

I knew I needed more than a rest. This hospital is a fine building in beautiful grounds with many trees and flowers. Inside is like a little town with shops, a bank and post office, a hairdresser and snackbar. The wards are large, but there are only six beds in each and the windows are big and look out on sky and hills. I had many tests and injections and medicines but I was worried all the time because mother got ill and said it was due to my going to hospital. I had to keep getting permission to visit her to try to cheer her up, telling her that there was nothing seriously wrong with me. The doctor told me that I must stop doing this as it was interfering with my treatment, so Mother must come to visit me.

22

One day Mother came to see me and I saw that she really was ill and not, as I had imagined, just worried and nervous about me. She confessed that she had been having pain in her stomach for some weeks but had not said anything, thinking it would go away. She agreed that evening to see a doctor and he told her she must go to hospital for tests. Poor Mother refused to go. She had always been distrustful of doctors, and was particularly frightened of injections. When I was a little girl and the 'injection people' came to the village, she would run away, even to another village, and take me with her. Neither of us ever had an injection, and of course I was as frightened of them as she was at first. By now I was quite used to them and hospitals and doctors and all, but Mother had not changed. When she learned that she would be in the same place as me she agreed to come, but she remained frightened all the time and kept asking to go home. I was able to spend plenty of time with her and this made it easier, but she was very ill and often in pain.

When the results of Mother's tests came through it was a terrible shock to us; she had cancer of the spine and it was incurable. The doctors told us she was going to die. Asha and I were so upset we could hardly believe it. Mother could not eat or drink without vomiting, so she was put on a drip; she was shrinking daily before our eyes, but she could still talk to us. The nurses liked her to have someone with her all day to translate for them, so we spent long hours at her bedside. At this same time I was told that medicine could not cure me and that I needed an operation for an ovarian cyst. I dared not tell Mother as she would be so worried for me, but perhaps it would have been better if I had, as she missed me so much and could not understand why I didn't visit her. I was so concerned for her that I hardly thought about my operation, and as soon as I was allowed up I went to see her. In those few days she had shrunk still more, her face fallen in and her arms like sticks.

Mother now knew that she was about to die. In India when someone is dying the close relatives never leave them, day or night; other relatives come and cook for them and do the work of the house. Mother did not understand that here it must be different. Asha was still at work, and I had my children back as soon as I left hospital. She kept saying, 'Don't you know what is happening here? Why do you go away? It is wrong and you know it. It is your mother who counts now.' Indeed it was, and every day I made the journey to hospital and sat beside the bed. I had been told to rest but this was impossible.

My family kept telling me that it was my fault that Mother was dying. Why else should she, who had always been so healthy, have become so ill? I was so upset by this that I began to believe them. One day while the children were still away I packed my bag and went to the hospital and told Mother that she must not worry about my future; I was willing to go back to my husband. My mother looked very distressed. Although she was so weak she roused herself and spoke quite loudly. 'No, no, never go back to him. He will kill you! Do what you like, divorce him and even marry again if you want to, but never, never go back to him. You are lucky to be free and have no man to worry you. Get a training, earn your own living and live your own life.' After this long speech she was exhausted. In this way my mother freed me from guilt. It was the last and perhaps one of the greatest services she did for me.

One day the doctor told us that they might be able to operate on Mother and that there was a fifty-fifty chance that she would survive. We agreed and hoped that if she was found to be very bad she would die under the anaesthetic and suffer no more. However she was so bad that the surgeon could attempt nothing and merely sewed her up again. All hope was then over. The last two weeks were so dreadful it is hard to have to bring them back, even after five years. Mother was taken off the drip as we were told this would only prolong her life, but it meant she had constant nausea as well as severe pain, and even a drop of water would cause painful vomiting of black blood. All the time as long as she could whisper to us she begged to be taken home, but we could not do this. The nurses came sometimes every hour to give her injections and prevent the worst sufferings. It was dreadful to deny her and we felt very guilty, as if we had betrayed her. I had to force myself to sit there hour after hour, just watching her suffer, when every part of me seemed to be struggling to escape. I felt ashamed that I stood it so badly, and I longed for her to die and release me as well as herself from the pain. Asha was much braver and more patient than I was.

One thing we could do for Mother was to pray and read from the holy book of the Master. He tells us not to be afraid of death, which must come to all of us, and not to cry for the dead, for death is release for them. We pray to God to bring us strength and peace. We believe in our sect that the Master will be waiting for us when we die, and will go with us to the judgement. Only those who have had many lives and have achieved great goodness, and have made the love of God the centre of our lives, will stay with God for ever. After Judgement most of us will have to take another body and live on earth again, perhaps as an animal if we have been bad in the last life. Mother had loved the Master all her life, and believed all that he taught; now she had his photograph in a frame on her bed-table, and her eyes kept turning to him, and her hands pointed towards him in prayer. I was afraid of death, and I still am, and of old age and sickness too. As a child, when I lay on the roof at night, I could see the fires in the distant cemetery and knew that the dead were being burned. I was afraid then, and even in daylight I would not walk near that place. Now that I had to face my own mother's death, both fear and sorrow were strong in me.

When we first knew that there was no hope for Mother we had written to Father asking him to come over here. We told him it was serious, but not that Mother was dying, and he had not yet arrived. We hoped he would not be too late. My sister Indira came, bringing her three little daughters, and as she was staying with me it was even more difficult to spend time with Mother. We told Mother that Father was coming as soon as we knew for sure, and although she could no longer speak she smiled. I think it was partly for me, as she was so sad to be leaving me alone. In India a young woman would never be on her own, and Mother thought that now I would be able to live with Father and have his protection. That was the last time I saw her alive. When we came next morning she looked peaceful in death, and although we cried we were glad. The photograph of the Master lay smashed on the floor. We knew that he had been in London and had left for home early that day. We said, 'He has taken her with him.'

In this country the Indian dead cannot be treated as they are at home. There a shallow pit is dug in the cemetery and prepared with wood. The corpse is washed and dressed – if a man, simply in clean white garments; if a widow, also in white; but if a wife, in the *salvar komise*, the tunic and trousers of the very best kind. She is made-up to look as beautiful as possible. The dead person is carried on a litter strewn with flowers and laid in the pit, surrounded with the fuel. Sandalwood and ghee are added for fragrance and good luck, and the priest says prayers and reads from a holy book. Sometimes a big earthenware pot is broken to show that a life is ended. The eldest son then lights the fire. If a woman has been widowed, she is taken to a place beside the water and there her bangles are broken and her make-up thrown away. In future she must dress in white, unless she has a son, and then she can wear light colours. The relatives and friends go back to the house and have a very simple meal, and for thirteen days they will come and sit with the family. On the third day they go to collect the ashes and these should be taken, if possible by the eldest son, to Hardvar, a holy town on the Ganges, so that the ashes can be strewn on the sacred water. The only difference in these customs is if a baby dies; then a shallow grave is made and the body covered with earth. The baby's clothes are laid on the grave, and it is very sad to see them there. I think everyone is afraid of the cemetery, as it is believed that ghosts and demons lurk there. Even if a good person dies the demons will be there, as he or she is sure to have done some evil.

Asha and Indira went to the mortuary to wash and dress Mother, but I could not bear to go. She had to be kept until Father came, and he arrived two days later. We all gathered at Asha's to greet him, and to our surprise he was very cheerful. He did not even ask about Mother, thinking, as we discovered later, that she was not really very ill but that we had invented this as an excuse for him to come over. We all looked at each other but no one had the courage to tell him the truth. Asha slipped out and went to Uncle Deen to ask him to come and help us. He told Father and they both cried. We all cried then, and tried to comfort Father.

Next day was arranged for the cremation, and the coffin was brought around to Asha's flat. But because it was two floors up, it could not be brought in, as is the custom, so that everyone might see the dead for the last time. Many people came to the funeral; I had not realised that mother had been so much loved. The owner of the factory where she had worked, all the workers, those who knew her at the temple, friends from the street and neighbourhood in addition to relatives, all came to say farewell to her. The coffin was opened at the crematorium, in the chapel so that all could see her; the priest said the prayers and it was over.

It has been very hard for me to go over my life like this; there are so many things I want to forget. I do not want to forget my mother, but her sufferings and the sadness in her life I do not want to bring up again. May she rest in peace.

23

Mother had left no money when she died, only a sewing
machine which was for me, some saris and a little jewellery.
Father had not much more than the clothes he had brought
with him, and although my eldest brother could have afforded
to pay for the funeral expenses, it is not the custom to ask
anyone in India for money. There the belief is strong that we
must all be very well off in Britain. Asha and Jasvinder paid
for the funeral. Afterwards we were together at their house.
Father had seen Mother's face when the coffin was opened
and he was shocked at the difference in her in only three
years. He had a photograph taken just before she left and he
showed it to us.

'Look at this,' he said, 'how young and well she was. What
did you do to her? You have killed her!'

Then he turned to me. 'It is all your fault. It is you who
have killed her!' he cried.

I could hardly speak I was so overcome by this unexpected
attack. But I knew how upset Mother would have been that
he should think this that I answered angrily.

'If anyone has killed her it is you,' I cried. 'Do you think I
have forgotten how you treated her, not just for three years
but for forty! She worked hard and you idled. I remember
how you used to beat her when she complained about your
idleness. My sisters and I cried and tried to stop you many
times; we will never forget.'

My father was astonished and tried to deny it, but of course
he really knew it was true. I could have said much more, that
often when Mother was working at a distant farm she had to
return late at night in the dark. The sewing machine was

heavy, she was tired, and it was not very safe for a woman to be out alone at night, but Father would not go to meet her. He was not tired, as he often spent the day in the village, sitting in the coffee shop. In spite of this, Mother respected him more than he deserved, but I did not. I certainly did not want him to protect me; he would be quite useless and I decided I would never live with him. He stayed with Asha and would help by taking the children to school. Since he is an old man now he is allowed to remain in this country, and although he often says he wishes he had never come here, he has never returned to India.

Of course Mother and the family had taken it for granted that I would have Father to live with me, and it would have been easier for me to be accepted by the community if I was once again be under the protection of a man. The fact that it would have to be *me* looking after *him* did not count. He spoke no English and was too old to learn and too set in his ways to adapt to the customs here. We were too far apart to share a life, and I would find him a burden and restriction. Perhaps the boys would too. The belief that a woman must always belong to a man made me angry. I had survived to have my freedom and I would not be stopped now. I had also to consider the money side: my Social Security was barely enough to keep me and the children, and I suspected that I would get little help from the other members of the family who could well afford it but always made out that I was well off. Father himself was not entitled to any pension, and although he soon proved he could make a little money by his tailoring it was not enough to keep him.

Poor Father, I feel more kindly to him now. He is old and lonely and in poor health. We have grown closer and I am more tolerant. Where at one time he mistrusted and criticised me for living alone he has at last come to respect me. One day he came to see me with a present of Indian sweets. 'For my son,' he said smiling. 'What do you mean?' I asked. 'You are like a son now, not a daughter, strong and independent. You have a good home and look after your children as if you were a man. I am proud of you.' This meant a great deal to me though I do not think it is a compliment to be called a man. From Father, it was a great compliment!

Indira meanwhile stayed on, being in no hurry to go back. Of all the family, even more than me, she is the unfortunate one. I remember her as a bright and happy girl, and very skilful at handicrafts she learned at college, but now she looked old and ill and shabby. She had given birth to four children in not much more than six years – the last three were daughters and unwanted by their father – and her health had broken down. At first her marriage had not been too bad, as her husband Akash had a job in London in a relative's shop, and they bought their own house. But this was shared with the mother-in-law, who made trouble for Indira, saying she had not brought enough dowry and that her son could have done better. Indira became pregnant, but she knew very little about such things, and when at seven months she had pains she thought that she had colic and went to the toilet. She was there for a long time, but no one took any notice until a neighbour heard groans and finally screams and broke down the door. He was horrified to find Indira unconscious on the floor, and a baby, still attached by the cord, in the toilet. I can never understand how this can have happened, but this is what I was told. An ambulance was called but it was too late; the child died on the way to the hospital.

After this Indira was unwell for a long time, but three years later she had a boy, and even the mother-in-law was pleased. In the next three years she had three more babies, all girls, and her health became much worse. She was quite unable to cope with all these children, especially as the eldest had nearly always been ill since birth. This gave the mother-in-law the excuse to take the boy away from Indira and bring him up herself, even while living in the same house. She kept him and fed him in her own room, and in time even prevented him from speaking to his mother and sisters. With such treatment from her mother-in-law, and contempt and cruelty from her husband, who often beat her, Indira became more and more helpless. Her place was in chaos, the children neglected, and two of the little girls were burnt or scalded because of her carelessness. It was not because she did not love them, or wished to neglect them, it was on account of

illness of mind and body. While I was still in London I called
to see Indira one day and found the eldest little girl screaming
in pain. She had pulled a pan of boiling water over her neck
and chest and was badly scalded. This had happened hours
ago, but nothing had been done. I picked her up and told
Indira to come with me to hospital. I did not know that I
could have called an ambulance, and we had to go to three
hospitals before we found one to take the poor little girl in.

When I came to Leicester Asha told me that Indira used to
phone her every week, begging for money and clothes for the
girls. Her husband had told her that she was ugly and useless
and that he did not want her or his daughters; she could go
away and take them with her. Of course she would have been
much better off without him, but was too disturbed to do
anything to help herself. The neighbours thought that she
was mad because they heard her banging her head against
the wall and groaning. When she phoned me later, I begged
her to go to a social worker and get help in sorting out her
life, but she was much too afraid of being blamed and of her
children being taken from her to confide in anyone. We did
arrange for a social worker to call but Indira would not open
the door. I understood, because at one time I had felt the
same. Indira was jealous of my having had so much help
from Mother, but there was little that Mother could do,
though she did go and stay with Indira several times. In the
end, after Mother had tried to protect Indira from Akash's
beatings, he forbade her to enter their house.

It was dreadful when Indira stayed with me: there were
nine people in my small flat, with the little girls – even the
eldest one of six years – all in nappies. And Indira was very
wasteful, too, which I could not afford. She would make
dozens of chapatis, more than we could possibly eat, and
most of them would be thrown away. It was the same with
everything she made, and I thought it no wonder the children were not properly fed. Although I wanted to spend as
much time as I could with Mother so that she might not feel
neglected, Indira kept pestering me to take her into town to
look at the shops. She had never been able to in London, and
became obsessed with this. It was as if she wanted to console

herself for the wretchedness of her life, as some people take to drink. She begged us all for money to spend, so that I who had so little for my own family had to give her more than I could afford. If she took a fancy to anything in my house or in Asha's she would put it away in her case. She even took Hernaik's school uniform and I had a lot of trouble getting it back. I had loved Indira in the past, but now she seemed like another person, unnatural and strange. It was a great relief when she went home, although we all sorrowed for her and her little girls. There seems to be no hope of happiness for them.

24

After Mother's funeral I found it difficult to go on living in the same way as before. I had complained about Mother at times, but now I felt guilty that I had. If only I could have her back! I still feel the same, I still miss her. She was the only person who really gave me love and cared about me. Even my children could not make up for her loss. At this time, too, several of my friends left the district partly because in the last three years our estate had been going downhill. This was some years ago, and for some reason other housing estates were also getting worse at this time. Vandals got busy and many of our local shops had to close; women were afraid to go out alone at night and children had to be kept indoors more. There were a number of break-ins in our block. The estate had a bad reputation when I first went there – that was why it was easy to get a good flat – but I had not been aware of it much at first.

When Asha and others began to tell me that I should move away and go back nearer to the Asian community I considered it seriously. There were not many Asians in that part of Chapleton and I might stand out too much and be attacked now that I was alone. A couple of men from the temple came to see me, saying it was not respectable for me to live alone and so far from my relatives. I expect they were afraid that without Mother to guide me I would go seriously wrong. They can never believe that I sleep alone; they imagine that I have lots of men in my life, and the fact that I am never even seen with men makes no difference. As they see it, a woman cannot live without sex. But I know only too well that I can, even if at times it is very hard: it used to make me angry when they thought this of me, but now I take no notice. Let them think what they like! I had found that as I became more confident and in better health men noticed me and wanted to get to know me, but I was not tempted. I still dreamed of my ideal man, kind, loving, generous and attractive, although I knew how hard it would be to find someone who would be kind to my children, too. After my experience of Indian men I tended to think that I could love a British man. In any case, no decent Indian man would want me; they usually like young unspoilt girls, preferably from home. The fact that I was pretty and slim and well dressed would make no difference to them.

I decided not to go back to Asha's street, or even to that district, as I resisted being drawn back in the community with its restrictions and gossip and the way I was made to feel like a nobody. My social worker found me a flat in a high-rise block not far from the city centre. It was one of many standing in a big bleak area, and I did not like it much: it was the only one on offer, and I took it without enough thought. The flat itself was quite good, and there were shops nearby: I could walk into town, and could get Indian food, which had been a problem. But this move proved to be disastrous. I had left the estate without realising the problems I would have to face. Social Security would not pay for this move, nor was I entitled to more household goods. I had left behind the carpets and lino as they were old and would not fit the new flat. My furniture was shabby and dirty and, worst of all, my cooking stove had been stolen; it had vanished during the move.

I had been told that high-rise flats were warmer, but we were desperately cold, and the only heating we had was one small electric fire in the big sitting room. We were cold in bed, too; the padded Indian quilts I had used before had been wet by the children in bed, and as they were too heavy to wash I had thrown them out. Now we had only a few thin blankets, so we snuggled together to keep warm.

It was only a few weeks since Mother had died, and I could not get over the sorrow of it. To make matters worse I had borrowed the two hundred pounds from Vilma, to pay for my passport, and I had to pay some back each week. I had learned to manage on my money, but this meant real hardship for the first time. I sank into despair; the flat was like a slum, there was no means of cooking and very little money. We boiled the electric kettle to make tea and ate cold food unless we went to my sister's place or to Vilma. How wretched it was. As on the estate I visited my neighbours and found a friend next door; she was an old lady suffering from arthritis, a Mrs Stroud, and when she heard that I had nowhere to cook she let me use her cooker. In return I shopped and did her housework and kept her company. About a week after our move, while Mrs Stroud was with me and the boys in our flat having tea, we were suddenly startled by a loud cracking noise. A stone clattered on to the bare boards through the window, which shattered right across. At the same time we heard a man shouting outside, so I ran and opened the door to the verandah and looked out. There was no one about but a fat man on a balcony nearby. When he saw me he started to shout again. 'Bloody Pakis and Blacks, we don't want them here. Get out!' Then more shouting and swearing. A woman passing below called up to him to stop. 'We all have to live,' she said. 'Leave her alone.' He took no notice. I was badly shocked and frightened, and asked Mrs Stroud if she knew who it was, but she said no.

Next day I went to the police to complain, and they sent two men to investigate. I had discovered that the man who had shouted was called Ed Boyd, a drunk who lived on the floor above us, but he was out and his wife swore he had done nothing. When they questioned Mrs Stroud she too said she had heard nothing. These two women were afraid, and so was I, all the time I remained at Elm Court, but no one ever stopped Mr Boyd, and he continued to threaten and abuse me and the children nearly every day. Sometimes at night I would hear him roaring and wait for his heavy footsteps to approach my door. Then he would beat with his fists and kick with his feet threatening to beat me up, while the children and I cowered inside feeling helpless. All this made me feel once more that the improvements I had made, all my efforts to be independent and brave, had come to nothing.

I could not move again; I could not make a decent home for my children, nor save them from fear and insult; I was a failure. I began to doubt that I would be accepted for British citizenship and then all hope would be over.

But once more a new hope came into my life. One day when I was visiting Mrs Stroud and doing her housework she had a visitor. It was Sister Magdalene, a Sister of Charity, who specially cared for the old and ill. I had always disliked the look of nuns, and if ever they came to my door in their black clothes with pale severe faces, I would not speak to them. They seemed like bad omens to me. Sister Magdalene was different, although she too was dressed in black and was pale. She was radiant and full of life and love. Her pale blue eyes were wide open like a child's, and though she must have been over sixty-five she was eager and lively like a young girl. She was thin and spare and did not look strong, but she seemed tireless; I was often to see her striding across the wide, littered wastes that surrounded the estate, probably carrying a couple of shopping bags in her hands. My friend told me once that she had been visiting a rather remote hospital and was driving into the road when she saw a little dark-clad figure standing on the pavement thumbing a lift. She recognised Sister Magdalene and stopped to pick her up. 'Did you know it was me, Sister?' she asked. 'Oh no,' said Sister, 'I am often obliged to do this; it saves so much time, and I meet so many nice people. Of course it is not very dignified, but I am sure the Lord will understand.' My friend thought it might be dangerous, but Sister never seemed to come to any harm.

The strange thing was that as soon as I saw her I was reminded of my mother. Although Mother was dark and brown-eyed, the very opposite of the pale Sister, they really were alike in some way. I knew I could trust her. It was in no way a part of her duty, but this did not matter to Sister: as soon as she realised that things were bad for me, she began to help. She looked into my eyes, took my hand and invited herself to tea. When she saw my place and my poverty and sadness, she became full of energy, and in a few days volunteers came around to redecorate the walls; then an old but quite good settee and armchairs arrived, as if by magic, and best of all a cooking stove. Even carpets and lino were found for me. Sister had taken us under her wing and it felt good, like having a mother again. Like a mother, too, Sister lectured me on looking after my house and being tidy and orderly, giving the boys regular meals and sending them to bed at the right time so that they could get up early in time for school. I was not very good at these things. It was so different back in the village: there we had plenty of space and very little furniture or ornaments. It was easy to sweep out rooms and wash floors and there were plenty of us to do the work. Our kitchens were very simple and we had only the most basic dishes, pots, pans and cutlery. Most of the time it was warm and dry enough for us to spend our lives out of doors. Here we are so often cramped into little flats, cluttered with possessions and having to cope with the weather and the dirt and dust of town. No wonder it is difficult!

In return for all her help I used to go with Sister to visit the old people she was so fond of, or take them on excursions or to tea parties. She knew I needed friends so she started to look out for young people whose company I would enjoy. She had so many friends they could not be counted. It was no wonder, for she spoke to everyone she met; it might be in a bus queue, or in a shop, or just passing in the street. She chatted and talked about her work to everyone, and spoke of the love of God as others spoke about the weather – as the most natural thing in the world. Somehow most people responded.

Gradually I told Sister my story, and she understood why I was often sad and depressed. She wanted me to be happy and confident, and though she believed that this would come through the love of God, she did not want me to give up the good things of life. She understood that I was a young woman who needed a man to love, and I could talk to her about this. 'Did you ever want a man, Sister?' I asked her once. 'I believe sex is beautiful when a man and woman love each other,' she answered, 'but of course I know nothing about it.' She looked at me and smiled. 'I knew even as a child that I was born to serve. This has been my happiness and my life.'

One Sunday we went with her to her church, and I liked it very much. The priest was dressed in green and gold, the candles were lit and there were flowers and statues. I remembered how I used to stand outside the hospital chapel when my sister was a nurse in India, and I would listen to the music and long to go in. I wondered why I was so strongly drawn to it, as if I belonged. The church was crowded, and after the service many people spoke to me and took my hand. After this Sister would tell me about Jesus and lend me books to read. She gave the children a big Bible with many beautiful coloured pictures too, but she told me that the most important thing for me was to love God and follow my conscience in my own religion, or any other. It was always the best she wanted for us. Now, four years later, I have still not made up my mind if I want to change my religion. I go to mass sometimes and I have some Catholic friends, and I should love to belong somewhere. I do feel remote from my own people, and I do not want my boys to grow up to be like many of the Indian men I know, with their way of life and their opinion of women as inferior to men – there to be of service and to do as they are told. Sometimes, though, I think of my guru and wonder if it is wrong for me to be disloyal after he received me and gave me the holy name. Perhaps he knows and is angry with me, and I will be unlucky. Then I remember that my own people and my own religion have not helped me or supported me in trouble.

Sister knew we had never had a holiday, so she arranged for us to stay together in a holiday home in the country and then, each year, for the boys to go to camp. Her many friends were always giving her money for good deeds, most of which went on the old and ill, but she had a few special people like me to help as well. I had a holiday in London, too, staying in the house of an Indian Catholic woman and her mother. It was wonderful to see the other side of London; they lived in Hampstead and I saw the big stores in Oxford Street, like Selfridges, the parks and the Commonwealth Institute.

One thing she could not do was help me to get away from

Elm Court. I loathed it more and more: the horrible man above us continued to threaten me, and I hated the lifts which seldom worked, and the dirty smelly passages and stairs. Everyone hates these places except the drunks and vandals and thieves who make them such a hell.

Two years had passed and I heard that my divorce had come through. I was given custody of the children, but Nirmal had the right to see them. I dreaded this, but at least I would not have to see him. The social worker arranged to call for the boys and take them to her office where Nirmal would call to collect them. I was afraid that he might try to snatch them away and take them to India, as does happen sometimes, but the social worker told me she would stay with them. When eventually Nirmal came and I told the boys that they were to see him, they were not keen to go; their memories of him were very bad. But they had no choice, and nor did I. Waiting at home for them to return I became very anxious when they were late. Nirmal had in fact invited the social worker to lunch with him and the boys; he spent freely, buying drinks as well, and had bought some toys for the children. When the social worker was telling me about it later she said she did not know why I had left him, he seemed so nice! He was wearing a very smart overcoat and had plenty of money. As usual he had been boasting to her. 'He still wants you,' she said. I thought how easy it had been for him to flatter her, and felt disgusted.

The next month Nirmal came again and brought presents that the children had asked for; a computer game for Koldeep and a watch for Hernaik. Again they went to a restaurant, which of course was a great treat for them, but when they said goodbye and Nirmal asked them what he should bring next time, Koldeep said, 'Please don't come back. We don't want to see you again.' He was always the one to speak out, although he was younger and such a little fellow. Nirmal looked at Hernaik, but he said, 'Me too. I don't want to see you either!' It was a surprise for me as well as for Nirmal, for though I knew my sons had every reason to dislike their father I had not expected them to do this on their own. Nirmal said he would come again next time nevertheless, and when the time came the social worker expected him. To our great relief he did not turn up, and the children have not seen him since.

Not long ago I heard that he had married again and was living in Birmingham. His wife was a young girl, brought over from India as I was, and I feel sorry for her. It is hard to imagine that Nirmal should have changed and could treat her kindly. They have a little daughter now and I am glad as this may make Nirmal forget my sons. I am often afraid that he might seek them out and try to influence them when they are older. Although we are very close now, and I know they love me, he still might be able to deceive them.

25

All this time I had been paying Vilma back the money I had borrowed. One day she phoned me to say that they had been burgled and lost a TV and video and other valuable things, but fortunately they were insured. I know that some people make claims for things that they never possessed; in fact I know several who have done this, and one even asked me to help, saying 'Everyone does it in this country.' I was a little afraid Vilma might ask me but fortunately she did not. Dishonesty upsets me; it seems to me that back in the village most people could be trusted. My mother was as honest as the day, and she used to say to me, 'If you steal even a sewing needle it is as bad as if it were a gold chain.' I said no I would not do it; even in this country it is still wrong. When I paid Vilma back it was with honest money.

Only once did I ever ask for help with money. Jasvinder and Asha had a very wealthy friend who was known to be very charitable, so one day when he was at their house I asked him if he would buy a little flat for me and my children. There was one for sale just nearby at less than two thousand pounds at that time. He refused me, saying, 'I will not encourage you to live alone. Go back to your husband and I will help you!' As he knew what sort of a man Nirmal was, and how I had been treated, I could say no more. Wealthy men like this will often help other men, however bad they are. I was told some time later that collections were being made for such a man in some country abroad. He had gone to live there and had done very well in business. His relatives, as often happens, started writing and sending messages, begging him to help them to join him there, so that they too could do well. He agreed as long as they would allow him to arrange to marry their children to the sons and daughters of his friends in the new country. They said they would, so he found jobs and accommodation for one family after another. However, one after another they arranged marriages without consulting him. He grew very angry and the third time it happened, he went to the wedding with a knife and attacked the bride. The bridegroom rushed to save her, but in the struggle he was stabbed through the heart and died. The businessman was charged with murder and money had to be collected for his defence. I do not know if this is true, but I felt bitter that a murderer can get help and sympathy, while a woman who has left her husband because of his cruelty gets none. It was silly of me even to ask.

Even the consolation of going to the temple and enjoying the festivals is now denied me. I cannot stand the way they look at me and ask me silly questions, and the women giggle. Even if I had left my husband but showed myself as humble and apologetic, accepting my low status, they would not have treated me so badly. The fact that I lived alone with my children and managed my own affairs made them both suspicious and jealous. How far this could go in meanness I will tell you. One day I went to the temple when there were gifts for all the women, but when they were handed out there was nothing for me. Hernaik went up to the woman who was in charge of them, although he was only eleven years old. 'Where is my mother's gift?' he asked. She did not answer so he took one of the parcels still left on the pile, thinking it had been a mistake. She snatched it back, saying, 'It is not for her.' Do you wonder that I seldom go to the temple now? Hernaik said, 'They do not respect you, mother.' It is bad for a child to see his mother humiliated.

However, without encouragement or help with money I did pay my debt to Vilma. You may wonder why my better-off sisters did not help me. My sister in Leeds whose family has a good business and two cars always insisted that I was very well off on Social Security and should be sending money back to India. My father thinks the same, but Asha, who is more realistic, and who does care for me, would help if she could. Asha rather envies me in some ways, because of my freedom. She does not follow tradition blindly and knows that you cannot live in Britain just the same way as in India. She no longer accepts that a woman should always belong to a man – first her father, then her husband, and if she has neither of these then to her brother or even her son. She would like to see the end of the dowry system and arranged marriages where the girl has no choice,. In all these things we agree. We are citizens of this country now, and do not intend to go back. We must make the best of it and hope these changes will come about. This is what Asha believes, but it is difficult for her to change, especially as her husband does not feel the same. When I hear of the things that go on in her family I am glad that I do not have such a husband, even a much better one than Nirmal. What little money I have I am free to spend as I like, but most married Indian women, even if earning a good wage, must give it to their husbands who make all the decisions. The white married girls I know seem to have more to say in their lives. Of course they complain to me about their husbands but their troubles are usually not as great as ours. I have been told that women here have had to fight very hard for their rights and to be more independent, and to some extent I think they have succeeded. Asha dislikes the dreary, overcrowded flat they live in and would like to move to a better district, but Jasvinder can never decide to move, even though they can well afford it. She would also like to have me and the children to her house more often, but he does not approve. I have their children at my place, and once I kept them for six weeks when they went on a visit to India. In return I was given a cheap dress that I could easily have bought over here.

I was fond of the two children, both younger than mine, especially Kanta the little girl. She is a sad-looking child, very thin and pale, and she has big thoughtful eyes. Billi is very quick and clever and much more confident. He is a great favourite with my two. Although Asha is more westernised than many Indian women Kanta is still treated very differently from Billi. Not long ago something happened that made me very aware of this, and very upset. Kanta was only seven at the time, and at school she had a 'crush' on a little boy about two years older than her. She would follow him around and give him little gifts bought with her pocket-money. The other children soon noticed and began to tease her; so did her brother, who told his parents too. There were dreadful scenes over this: Kanta was beaten and terrified by her father. He said, 'You have disgraced the family. You are shameless and no man will ever be willing to marry you. Never speak to that boy again.' Poor Kanta became even thinner and paler. She was in disgrace for a long time and made to feel guilty and ashamed, as if she had committed a terrible sin.

When she comes to see me she wants to sit on my knee. She kisses my hands and even my clothes, saying, 'I love you Auntie Sita.' Once she said, 'I do not often see Mummy, she is always at work and I do not like my Daddy.' I know she is in great need of more love, and that perhaps is why that little boy was so important to her. It is not Asha's fault; she cannot escape easily from our customs, and she dare not oppose her husband too much. I suppose she even loves him; at any rate, she makes him the centre of her world. Lately she has been helping me more than ever before. She would like me to have a chance in life, and will help me if she can. I am very grateful to Asha now, especially as I feel once again that she loves me.

It was a real thrill when I got my British citizenship, and could feel secure in this country. I had a little more to spend and was wearing skirts and dresses instead of old sweaters and jeans. I seldom put on my Indian clothes now, unless I am going somewhere special, for the sari is like evening dress. I love to look fashionable and have the boys well dressed too. Then I decided to join a health club, as many of my friends did. There are several in the city, some very expensive and beautiful, but mine is cheap, and every year I stay I have to pay less. Many of the members are pensioners who enjoy the company and the sauna and jacuzzi: some like me are mothers or unemployed. We always go during the day, but those who work go in the evenings or at weekends when it is more crowded. I do exercises in the gym and attend classes in movement and dancing; I have saunas and have a shower which saves hot water at home. It is good to feel fit, and I even like the walk there and back, which I really take to save the fare. It is quite a long way, so I am getting stronger all the time.

Some day I hope I will be able to work and come off Social Security, but as Sister says I must put my children first, look after them, see that they are well fed and happy and have a mother waiting for them when they come home from school. In any case, it would be hard for me to find a job that would pay me as much as I get now, as my rent and rates are paid and I get many things free. Meanwhile I have a very small job from the Social Work Department, visiting old people. I have only to stay and talk to them, or take them out, and report back if they need additional help. Friends often give us good meals, take us on outings and give presents to the children. We live very simply at home, eating healthy food like wholemeal bread and flour, lentils and beans, brown rice, and plenty of greens and other vegetables. It is more like our food back in India. The boys have eggs and meat sometimes. They do not like curries. Hernaik loves cooking and is very good at it – much better than I am, although he is only twelve. His cakes and scones are always light, and he keeps learning new dishes from the cookery books. My friend thinks he will perhaps be a chef, or manage a restaurant or hotel. I should like this, as I do not want him to go and serve in a shop as many children do if they are not very clever at school. I think he is clever enough to go to a college to learn about catering and cooking. Koldeep does not know what he wants to do; he is very sociable, always makes friends easily and seems to amuse people. He is still small, and although bright and quick, is young for his age too. It is sad for them to have no father, but better no father than a bad one I tell them. They think the same. My own father is still irresponsible. When he comes to see us he always brings a big bag of sweets and biscuits and cakes, although I have told him often that it is bad for the children and I would much rather have fruit or fruit juice for them. It is a lonely life here for him, I know, as he has never learned any English. He sleeps in the kitchen at Asha's, and when he gets tired of them he goes to my sister in Leeds. Sometimes he will sit in for me so that I can go out at night, but we do not get on well and he is easily offended. There is much more than the usual gap between parents and children: there is a culture gap as well.

26

Sister Magdalene found a special friend for me, an elderly lady who had been a teacher but is now retired. She was doing voluntary work helping disabled people with their education, and Sister asked her if she would help me with my English. I can talk freely, but not very well: I make mistakes and do not know enough words; this shows up when I am trying to write. This lady became like another mother to me, and her husband and daughter are like my family. They take the greatest interest in the boys, take them out, and have them to stay. I did not seem to make much progress with my English, so to get me to talk more carefully, Mrs Barton said one day, 'Tell me about your life in India, Sita.' I started, and she was so interested she said, 'Shall I write it all down as you tell me? Perhaps it would even make a book and be published. There can be no harm in trying, and in any case it will be interesting to many of our friends and relatives in Britain. It will also explain things in your life for your children to read when they are old enough to understand.' So that is how our book came to be written. Mrs Barton would take notes as I spoke; then write it out in full and read it back to me. By now many people have read it, including two novelists, and one specialist on Indians in Britain, and we were very pleased to know that they read it with interest.

Sometimes I feel very homesick and long to go back to my village and all the familiar places I knew as a child. I should love to travel through India: go on the trains, visit my relatives in different parts, but I may never have the chance, at least until my sons are grown up. Krishna, my eldest brother, has offered to pay my fare, but he cannot afford to pay for the children too. All the same, I would not wish to live in India again. Britain is now my home, and with all its faults I want to stay. It has much to offer us and I am grateful.

There are many turning points in life; in mine, at any rate, some big and some small. One small but important one came when Mrs Barton said when I first met her, 'You have a beautiful face, Sita. Many artists would like to paint or sculpt you.' I was astonished. I had never been told such a thing before. She explained that I had a good bone structure in my face, and that my features were well formed: I had a lovely smile and expressive eyes. At first I thought that she was just saying this to give me confidence, but her daughter who is an artist said so too. After this I really did feel good; I walked with pride and held my head high.

As I go about the city I hear men whistle after me; in the shops they try to chat me up. If I go with a girlfriend to a café some man will want to get to know me; no one would guess that I don't have a boyfriend, but these men are not the kind I am looking for. At twenty-eight, although I had two big children, I was like a young girl without experience. I had never been kissed. One day I was introduced to a young man who was a teacher; lonely like me, and like me divorced. For some weeks I went out with him, to the films, to restaurants, to bars where he drank beer and I had orange juice. I even went to meet his family who were quite well off; they were very kind and friendly. He used to take me home in his car, but I never invited him to my home or let him see my children. I did not yet trust him. When we said good night he always wanted to kiss me, but for a long time I was too shy. I was so curious, though, that at last I did, and I did enjoy it; not as much as I had hoped, because I was not in love with him. I would never let him go further, even to touch my breasts, which were now shapely again. He said he understood how I felt, but of course he grew tired of waiting, and we drifted apart. I was not sorry, nor was I sorry that I had known him and had my first kisses; it made me feel more like a woman.

A big change was to come into my life, more important than this and quite unhoped for. I managed to leave that horrible Elm Court, where we were still being threatened by the drunken man upstairs. Hernaik was beaten up by bigger boys in the lift and was badly frightened and friends did not like to visit us at night. One day I happened to see a notice in a shop window advertising for a swap of a fifth-floor flat for a larger one lower down. It was hard to believe that anyone would choose to live at Elm Court, but I went around to see the other flat, which was in an old building. The entrance and stairs were clean, and there were only ten flats. This one was small – the sitting room and the two bedrooms especially – but everything was fresh and modern and the kitchen and bathroom were nice. The couple who lived there had one child and were expecting another, and this space was no longer suitable for them; when they heard where I lived they were actually pleased, because by a lucky chance her parents lived in the same block. We soon agreed to swap and this time it was a good move for me. Sister Magdalene helped us with the move, and this time I had no worries as the carpets and lino were all left for us. Vilma and her husband were refurnishing their house and they offered me some things they did not want. They were in good condition and nice as well. Thus I have a lovely new double bed with duvet and sheets to match, a wardrobe and dressing table, and in the sitting room a fine cabinet. Other friends gave me presents for the house and for the first time I could be really proud of my home.

That first year in South Street was a good one. I would not say my neighbours were friendly, but they did not worry us. The shops were nearer and the district, though not posh, was better. We were now quite close to a canal, and when Mrs Barton saw this she said that the boys must learn to swim. Every now and then a child gets drowned there, especially when there is ice and it gives way. She found a club where they could learn, and every week a mini-bus came to pick them up and take them to the swimming bath. Of course they loved this, were not at all afraid of the water. In a short time they could swim.

That spring Sister said we should have a holiday, but she could only offer us fifty pounds towards it. She always had trouble with her conscience, wondering how to divide up what she's been given among so many of her friends. Her real job, of course, is with the old and ill, but she cannot resist trying to help every person she meets who also needs help. I think Sister has a special love for me, as I have for her, but I suppose there are others who think the same, because it is her way to care so much. She is cheerful, funny sometimes, and she talks too much, but she seems to carry a light round with her; I think it is love.

I asked Mrs Barton about the cheapest way to get a holiday and she said, 'A holiday camp, of course.' She had never been to one but she knew all about them, and she explained that there are no extras. All meals and entertainments are included in the cost, and you never need to leave the camp. There are special people to look after and amuse the children, so parents can feel free. I started to save up, but in the end I had to borrow some more money from Vilma. Sister went to the special office in town and persuaded them to take ten per cent off the price of the holiday and to give us free coach travel both ways. We were all very excited, as this would be the first real holiday we had had, not a charity one, or staying with friends. I wanted to have some nice summer clothes to take, but by now I had become so clever at picking out bargains that it was no worry and I enjoyed it too. My sister and some of her friends would keep coming to see what I had found at jumble sales and charity shops and begging me to give some to them. I usually did, as I could not resist a bargain and often I bought more than I needed, and this had become a hobby. I would say to them sometimes, 'Why don't you come to the jumble sales with me?' They were much too proud!

At last the day came for us to go. It was early in August. We said goodbye to everybody as if we were going for a month to India, but it was only for a week and about a hundred miles away.

27

My story started in a village and I shall end it in another. You may think it very strange that I should find my Indian village and a holiday camp in Britain alike in any way, but to me they were. The home village was full of life and people were mixing together all the time. There was always something happening, perhaps an engagement party, a wedding, a religious festival, or even a funeral, and everyone to some extent took part. On the happy occasions we dressed in bright clothes, wore flowers, made music, sang and danced. There was plenty of delicious food, and even if one was not invited there was sure to be food over. At night on festive occasions there were bright lights; in the daytime the sun was usually shining. This is the happy side of life as I remember it from my childhood. I liked too our closeness to the open country-side, the trees that shaded the village, and the clear water flowing.

When we arrived in the holiday camp the weather was good, and the holidaymakers were bustling about in their summer clothes, looking bright and cheerful in the sunshine. They seemed very friendly and lively, enjoying themselves as they went to the different entertainments. There was music everywhere, and I soon found you could dance most of the day and night if you wanted to. There were shops of every kind in the Centre, and bars and cafés and discos; two swimming pools, inside and outside, and a funfair for the children. When we were taken to the chalet it was in a quiet place, surrounded by grass and flowers and trees, like the country. I was delighted with my first sight of all these things. Our chalet had one room with three beds, a wardrobe and a dressing table, and we had our own little bathroom. Everything was very clean and I found later that a domestic lady came twice a day, morning and evening to look after it.

We were tired from our journey that day, so we all had baths and then went to the dining room. We were not far from all the places in the Centre, but there was a lovely little train, like a big toy, that took us here and there to different parts of the camp. The boys were very excited when they saw this. The dining room was a beautiful big place crowded with people. We shared a table with an elderly couple, Mr and Mrs Martin, who were kind and friendly. When I told the waiter that I was a vegetarian the supervisor himself brought me a lovely salad; he did this at every main meal, and I had many different kinds of salads while I was there. We went to bed early that night so as to be fresh in the morning. We slept well as it was very quiet where our chalet was.

Next day we went exploring, and soon found the funfair which was marvellous for the children as they could go on the roundabouts, dodgems, aeroplanes, and many other things, all free. Later we found they could also paddle canoes on the lake, play snooker and table tennis, miniature golf and pitch and toss as much as they liked. I was able to leave the boys in the care of the red-coats and go wandering about myself, looking at everything and everybody. I was glad I had a nice sundress and sandals and could fit in with the crowd. Everywhere I went I was surprised to see that there were no Asian people at the camp; in fact I saw only one Indian woman on one day. I soon found the gymnasium and joined a movement class. I enjoyed this very much and had a chance to talk to other girls and older women, but after a while I began to feel a little sad because I seemed to be the only person alone. There were many couples, both old and young, or families, or parties of friends. My children were quite at home; they were busy playing all day with many new friends and could hardly bear to sit through meal times. That evening I went to the disco after the children were in bed. It was a beautiful place with a good band and lights and colours. I felt shy at first, going in alone, but I soon had partners; the first was the supervisor who brought me the salads, but he was a bit old. There were plenty of young men and I had a wonderful time, dancing until two in the morning.

Next day I was again on my own, but after the mid-day meal when I was talking to Mrs Martin she said, 'There is a beauty competition today Sita, my husband and I both think you should enter. We believe you should win.' I felt very pleased that they should think this, but frightened too. However, after some persuasion I did decide to try. The competition was for the loveliest dress, and here I had a great advantage as I had brought one of my saris. It was a beautiful one in vermilion silk, richly embroidered with gold. My mother had left it for the wife of her eldest grandson, but as his marriage was very far away, Asha who was keeping it gave it to me. It was very different from the cheap nylon sari my mother-in-law had given me. I did my hair carefully and put on my gold jewellery and I knew I looked good. One of the receptionists, a nice friendly girl, gave me advice on how to walk on the stage and told me to smile at the judges. When I arrived at the hall there were eleven other girls and the compère told us what we must do. He gave us a little rehearsal first so that we knew where to walk and in what order, and how to hold the cards with our numbers on. I think we were all nervous but I was the most nervous of all because it was so strange to me. When we had to face the audience and the judges it was worse still, but I gradually plucked up courage and when the compère asked me questions about myself I spoke up. When I said I came from Leicester there was a big cheer, as so many of the audience came from there too. I felt I must have won as no one else got a cheer, even if they did come from Leicester and I could not help knowing that my outfit was much more striking than any of the others. At last the judges decided and the compère called out a number. It was not mine, and my heart sank. I tried to go on looking cheerful, but my heart beat as he called out the second number; still not mine. Then my number was called at last, and I went up to receive my prize, so disappointed that I was not even smiling. The judge kissed me and congratulated me, giving me a pretty silver cup, and everyone clapped very loud. Before I could say a word I was taken into the garden to be photographed. There were three photographers all asking me to do this and that and smile, while a reporter from the local newspaper asked me questions. I was quite bewildered. That night I went dancing, and everybody wanted to know me and talk to me, men and girls too. I could hardly believe it.

Next day at breakfast Mr and Mrs Martin asked me to tell them about the competition as they had not been able to attend. Well, I said it was very nice, but I only came third. How they laughed! 'You silly girl, do you really mean to say that you did not know you were first? Of course you won the competition as we said you would!'

Then I laughed too and felt very happy. I had no idea that the winning number is always given last! Mrs Martin then told me that there was another competition that day too, and was for make-up. 'You must try that too, Sita,' they said. Why not, I thought, I will enjoy doing it again. This time I went to the hairdresser for a special style. Everyone said it looked lovely. The friendly girl who had helped me before advised me on make-up; another lent me a smart bag to go with my summer dress, and I even had a gold watch and necklace lent to me too. This time I did not expect to win as there was a girl much younger than me, very pretty, and dressed in a lovely white outfit. She did win, but I came second and went up to win another smaller silver cup. Again I was photographed many times, and felt much more relaxed. I noticed one of the photographers more than the others. He was very tall and broad-shouldered and had thick dark hair. I liked his looks and especially his nice grey eyes. I kept seeing him look at me, and when he took my photo he made me smile. His name was Nicky. At the disco that night he asked me to dance and kept the other partners away. I did not mind, as he was the most attractive man in the camp; he could have had any of the girls, but he wanted me.

The next few days went quickly. I had plenty to do and many new friends. Some asked me to go and visit them after the holiday, or to write and keep in touch. The fifth day was the most important as the big competition took place then.

This was for 'Miss Holiday Princess.' There were posters advertising this and a big board on the stage in the hall. I did not need to be told to go in for this one, I was quite determined to try, though I did not think I would win if the pretty girl who'd won the make-up competition was to enter. Lucky for me she had gone home! I put on my prettiest dress, shoes, the best I had, and got ready. A family I had been friendly with invited me to have a glass of white wine with them and I tried it; the first I had ever tasted. It made me feel as light as air and very happy! Fifteen girls entered this time, all younger than me, between about sixteen and twenty-four. Everyone was surprised when I said my age, and I began to feel doubtful. However, I knew I must not show this so I smiled and walked confidently. Waiting for the judges to decide is always painful. There were six of them this time, and a larger audience. This time I was glad when I did not hear my number called out first and second. Yes I really was the winner! I went up smiling this time to receive my prize; a silver necklace and earrings in a pretty box, and I enjoyed the cheers and congratulations. The photographers were busy as before and Nicky was as pleased as I was.

That evening I went dancing as usual, and even tried another competition for disco dancing. I did not expect to win but I came third. I danced with many partners; even the band leader came to ask me, but at last I felt tired and sat down surrounded by my friends. Suddenly Nicky came running in. He had finished his work and showered and changed into a fresh white shirt. Without a word he took my hand and pulled me to my feet, and tired no longer I ran out with him into the garden and the cool night air. For a while we walked together hand in hand talking and laughing. Then we went to one of the bars, a beautiful place where there were real trees and flowers and running water like a stream. I could not understand how there seemed to be clouds and rain, like nature, or like magic. We danced and the evening passed, until hot and tired once more we ran out of the camp and down to the sea and the wide empty beach. I had never been there before. It was wonderful to see the soft waves coming in and feel the cool breeze; even the moon was there! It was the first time Nicky and I had been alone together. He put his arms round me and kissed me and told me he loved me. I held him tight and kissed him back. It was a wonderful end to a wonderful day, like a dream or a love story.

I will never forget being Holiday Princess on that day. Here was I, Sita, an Indian village girl. It was only a few years since I had been beaten and starved; I had been near to death even. Nirmal and his family had despised me; when I left him my own community treated me as nothing, a woman no one wanted to know or to help. They thought I was mud, I said to myself, but under the mud was gold!

Epilogue

Now, more than a year later, I look back on my life since that happy moment. Nicky was not the man for me; he was much too young and irresponsible. When I returned home he used to phone me every evening, and one day he turned up on my doorstep. I told Sister and she found him a room quite nearby to stay in. He went to Social Security and they paid for it. He tried to get a job, but as he had no qualifications or training, and was not even an experienced photographer, he did not succeed. It made me realise that he was childish and even a bit of a scrounger. His good looks and charm had helped him to get through life without effort. I did meet his parents and we got on well. They invited me and the children to stay and they were kind, but it could not last between Nicky and me, though I did care for him, more than any other man I had known since I said goodbye to Rama. I never see him now.

Occasionally I will go out with a man friend, just for a change, no more. Now I am more serious and realise that the admiration of men and beauty competitions and fashionable dress are not all that important to me. I must put my sons first until they are older. What man, Indian or British, would care for them? What man would they accept? I will still be young enough when they are grown up to find true love and marriage. I will not put all hope of this out of my heart.

Another hope is to be an independent woman earning my own living in a way that I enjoy. This too is possible because kind relatives and friends helped me to get a training as a hairdresser. I worked hard and passed the exams. Now I am very proud of the two framed diplomas that hang on my wall.

I will not pretend that my life is all easy now. I worry about my sons growing up between two cultures and belonging fully to neither. Hernaik is doing well at school and talks now of going to a university. Then I will be proud. Koldeep is still very much a child, full of life and fun and seeing nothing as serious.

Sometimes too I feel that the damage done to me in the dreadful years of my marriage has killed something in me. I find myself saying 'I am done for, I am done for' and everything seems dark and difficult as the memories come back. It is then I feel dependent, almost as a child is, on my friend and her family and Sister Magdalene. I am sad that she is now far away from Leicester, recalled to other work by her Order. She is missed by many others besides me, I know. Occasionally I see her and she gives me love and strength. When Sister read this book, one of the things she said was, 'I know, Sita, that you have been very unfortunate in the men you have known in your life, but I know too there are many good Indian men in this country who love their wives and children. They work hard to provide for them and practise their religion. Of course, I know more about the Christian Indians, some of them priests, and they are very good men.' I agreed with Sister. My experience has been very limited and what she says must be true to hers. She has had a long life and known many people.

This book came to be written by chance, but as I unfolded the story of my life I began to see purpose in it. It helped me to tell someone who cared and sympathised; it helped me to get my ideas clear about what had happened to me. Some Indians will say that I am betraying my own culture and my own relations and friends from home, or they will think I am blaming the custom of arranged marriages for my sad life. I am not against arranged marriages if they are done with care, if there is no greedy grasping for dowries, and if the young people are allowed their part in the choice of a partner. I think some British girls I know would be glad to have the chance of a marriage arranged in this way. For Indian women like me, on their own after divorce or being widowed, there is little chance of re-marriage. We are outside the system, and however good we might be as wives, however loving and honest and attractive, Indian men do not want us. There are exceptions, of course, and an especially big dowry might help. Also if a girl over here can offer an Indian man the chance to come to Britain as her husband she will probably find someone. Even I could, I expect, but I would be afraid the man might pretend to love me but just make use of me and leave me after marriage. Perhaps I have become too suspicious and frightened, but this is how life has made me.

All the same I still love the good things in my culture; they are precious to me although I feel myself now almost an outsider. I also love the freedom and independence that being in Britain has given me; the friends, the opportunities for my sons, the opportunity to be myself.

The bad things I have told about my own people are true. It is time Indians faced the truth. No woman should be treated as I was treated and left to suffer, beaten, terrified and alone, childhood and girlhood lost in a strange world. Neither my community nor my religious group could tell me more than to let myself be destroyed. I believe that as long as men are made to feel, even from babyhood, that they are great and important and women are of a lower order, just there to serve them, they will be corrupted. Such ideas lead to evil and both men and women are degraded by them. Only a few, like my mother, can rise above it all. She was the clear star in my life.

It is no use looking for causes outside ourselves and blaming others. It is we who are to blame and only we can change things. If this book, the story of my life so far, can help in the smallest way to make this change come about, it will give more meaning to my life. I have changed a great deal and learned much, but deep down in me, from the days when I was happy and innocent, there is still the heart of an Indian village girl, and still the longing and the hope that there will be, some day, more love in the world.

Afterword

Yasmin Alibhai
& Pragna Patel

The story of Sita is an intensely personal one. It is also a story which evokes the tormented life experiences of many Asian women living in this country, and the particular pile of coercive structures (including many contradictions) that forces them continue in the lives of misery in which they find themselves. It is not the story of all Asian women, in spite of the impression that might be gleaned from the ceaseless media processing of harrowing tales of arranged marriages and the plight of the 'poor' Asian woman, forever a victim to be pitied and rescued by nice white people. Asian women are fighting back. Ultimately, this is also a story which crosses all boundaries, because male violence to women does not restrict itself to any one race, community or economic group. In this Afterword, we connect these three and discuss the milieu around these kinds of tragic, individual situations. It is, in one sense, lamentable that an Afterword of this kind needs to be written at all, but we live in a racist society where, as yet, there is both scant understanding and a willed ignorance of the lives of black people, and all too often the experiences of people like Sita are used to feed the spectres of horror at the 'barbaric black' that reside (sometimes at a subconscious level) in the minds of most white British people. Perhaps this is one of the deeper injustices black women suffer. They are denied that most basic human right, to speak subjectively about themselves without becoming 'typical' of their race and sex.

By its very nature, domestic violence is a difficult subject to discuss openly and dispassionately. It has a subterranean life, and like incest and child abuse, it is protected by that hard shell, a corporate belief in the sanctity and autonomy of family life. This belief, in the case of domestic violence, is sanctioned by the law and society and it is a code night-marishly difficult to break. There is the double-glazed privacy and tacit morality which forbids the washing of dirty linen in public, especially, it seems, if it is bloodstained. As it is a taboo subject, those who know and those who suffer are forced to collude in these indoor games of obfuscation. Until they can't or don't.

For Asian people who live always with racism, this secrecy becomes even more imperative, and silent acceptance is demanded in the name of solidarity and strength. For black Asian women who are fighting against male violence, the racism adds a further complexity to their struggles. They have to fight a society which on an institutional level denies them and theirs the right to decent housing, schools and employment and, on an individual level, abuses and attacks them. For most black people the dream of a 'Great' Britain which would open a door of golden opportunities has been shattered. Racism and racist attacks have exploded the well-instilled myth of the benign white colonial. Black people are thus constantly having to challenge the institutions of the state – the police, Home Office, and so on – and often on matters of basic survival. For many black women the central battle is against racism, and the enormity of that struggle often forces other serious issues to take a back seat or dis-appear altogether. Serious thought needs to be given to the complexity of waging struggles against both racism and sexism. For example, many practices and traditions go un-challenged within the community which legitimise the subordinate role of women and confine them to that sphere of life – the family – where control is absolute and difficult to defy for fear of lending ammunition to the white society. If it is now recognised that Asians live under greater stress as a direct result of racism and suffer higher rates of heart attacks than might be expected, similar pressures – for example, a higher rate of unemployment – are contributing factors to eruptions at home. These factors have prevented women from leaving home in the past.

Now, the conspiracy of silence is breaking and the scene is rapidly changing as more and more women are coming out into the open and demanding redress. This is not because more women are suffering, but because an increasing number are taking decisions to reshape the pattern of their unhappy lives. Asian women have a long history of struggle against brutality. In India, violence to women is one of the key issues to which the Indian women's movement is addressing itself. Here in Britain too the most trenchant and direct action against domestic violence has been initiated by Asian women's organisations, and these strategies have been emulated by other women's groups. This indicates the level of politicisation and self-organisation that exists in the British Asian community. Organisations like the Birmingham Black Sisters and the Southall Black Sisters have provided practical lifeline support for women and have tirelessly campaigned for a change in social and community attitudes towards this appalling crime. When a young woman, Krishna Sharma, was found hanged after years of abuse at the hands of her husband, the Southall Black Sisters and other groups picketed outside the family home to show their repugnance and publicly to shame the family. It was an effective and unique strategy to use in a community highly conscious of its social image. It was an extraordinary occasion to see predominantly Asian women, some as old as sixty years, carrying banners and shouting that enough was enough, that a woman had a right to live her life in safety and peace.

Very public responses to something considered so utterly private, these high-profile (highly dangerous) activities are beginning to affect the community. Fighting back against domestic violence means tackling basic structures like extended families and also the cultural concepts that lie behind those structures. In the Asian community the notion of 'Izzat' or honour is an extremely powerful precept prevalent in all major Asian religions. It is central to keeping women under control and within the confines of the family. Women are the upholders of the honour of their own family and that of their in-laws. If a woman chooses to deviate from the norm, by choosing her own partner in marriage, marrying outside her caste or religion, or separating from her husband, she commits the ultimate crime. She dishonours her families, her culture and religion. She is considered guilty of bringing shame to the household and is treated as an outcast. She is denounced and labelled 'bad'. She is often regarded as coming under the influence of western (immoral) values which have had a corrupting influence on her. The minute an Asian woman steps outside her prescribed role, she is seen as tainted, promiscuous and degenerate and is therefore treated with contempt by the community. Her children also bear the stigma of her actions. Her open defiance of certain aspects of her culture is seen as a total rejection of her roots. That the reasons for her actions may have some validity are not examined. Her actions, not their causes, are the sole focus of attention for the community.

In cases where women have marital problems, community leaders, mainly men (like all bishops and other custodians of virtue) from the religious institutions, the temples, gurdwaras and mosques, come together and hold a series of 'reconciliation' meetings – rejecting outright the outside agencies like the courts. The sole purpose of these meetings is to ensure that the woman is rounded up and put back into her pen – that the status quo is maintained. The woman is often blamed for not having a strong enough moral constitution and having too low a tolerance threshold. She is warned not to defy their rules and thus cause further dishonour. There leaders have a vested interest in ensuring that the women do not defy their rules and laws and, by implication, their authority and rights as community spokesmen.

These are, of course, always poetic images and ideals that are promoted to back and sustain iniquities. The ideal Asian woman, much eulogised in popular Indian films, is long-suffering, obedient, passive. She carries out her role of dutiful mother and wife and this is her only pleasure and happiness. She herself has no desires (and especially not sexual desires). She is meant solely as an object for the satisfaction of others. To suffer in silence is virtue and goodness. It is important not to react to this with gory anthropological fascination or unthinking outrage reserved for 'alien' customs, or with patronising reforming zeal. Except for a few specific cultural details, the picture in this country for pre-war women was almost identical. Nor is this a sign that these 'aliens' are behind and only need time to catch up with the civilised way of things. Femininity in this country, under the thin veneer of equality, is still very much defined in terms of passive sweetness. Look at the attitudes towards male and female promiscuity. Marriage is a gamble whatever the mode and there are unhappy relationships in the Asian community as there are in the white community. And one pressure many Asian families don't have is the Barbara Cartland romantic expectations of champagne and roses. The extended family can be supportive in this hostile environment, but it is also oppressive to women. Not all Asian families are tyrannical, not all white British families are not. And not all Asian girls are, in the infamous and immortal words of the salubrious *Daily Mail*, 'birds in cages'.

In their fight for freedom, Asian women sometimes face opposition from other women who uphold the traditional values of the community. Ironically, those who are oppressed often become overzealous colluders with that system of oppression: black policemen beat up black children in South Africa and many women in parts of Africa fight to retain female circumcision. For more homespun examples, you need only look at the degree of female disapproval when a 'mother leaves her children' and at the fact that whatever the real cause of separation between a couple, it is the women who is left feeling more guilty than the man.

In the face of these powerful deterrents, the stakes are very high indeed when women do ask for help. They need to be, and are, very brave, because in breaking the silence they know they will be ostracised by the community and their families. Some make several attempts to leave and go back; others have the notion of 'Izzat' so deeply imbedded that they choose suicide rather than disgrace. What awaits them is equally frightening: isolation in a racist white society, lack of awareness of their rights, and a legacy of rejection which they pass on to their siblings and children. And in spite of all this, at the centres run by Asian women for Asian women which have sprung up all over the country, business is still pretty good.

Obviously, the more reactionary elements of the community do not see these centres as a godsend. Centre and refuge workers have gathered around them a mythology of evil. They are 'prostitutes', home wreckers and are frequently accused of breaking up homes and community structures. These are general societal attitudes – white refuge workers have similar accusations hurled at them. Speaking out against male violence is in effect speaking out against the subjugation of women which the community has for centuries legitimised through religious and cultural justifications. But whilst the community, in the fight against racism, expects to come together, it will not do the same on issues of male violence to women. It is in reality a shabby bargain.

The workers at these centres have developed unique ways of working. They are in there with the women who come in. They have clearly defined their role as primarily working to provide a safe environment for the victims, whatever that takes. They have accumulated a vast amount of experience in dealing with lawyers (in fact there is a network of sympathetic lawyers who provide voluntary advice on their books), housing offices and the DHSS. They network with each other and challenge the system on behalf of the very vulnerable women who come to them, often by playing an advocacy role and demystifying preciously guarded 'professional' positions and incomprehensible laws which deny rights through creating mental confusion. By highly organised interference they get things done: they have redefined the established (western) boundaries of advice work. The Asian women's refuges also reflect this co-membership and genuine bond of purpose between the users and the workers.

Other wider issues underpin attitudes towards domestic violence. There is the prevailing sexist world view that women who are violated are responsible in some way for what happens to them, like rape victims ticked off in court by 'impartial' judges for dressing too attractively or presuming to walk after sunset. There have recently been court cases in which the defence has justified the killing of a wife by a husband on the grounds that she nagged the poor man until he had no choice but to do away with her. In a case involving an Asian man who had murdered his wife, the defence made a distinction between murder (for money) and domestic murder (the latter less serious). The dangerous view that marriage bestows proprietal rights on a man over a woman is never hard to find, east or west. These beliefs go deep and women internalise them too. In Birmingham, when an Asian woman protected herself from a brutal attack by her husband and, after a lifetime of abuse, caused his death, the commu-nnity on the whole did not offer any support because it was felt that this would legitimise the right of women to defend themselves. It was the women's organisations which carried out a long and arduous campaign against the trial, which they felt was racist and sexist, and after three years obtained something resembling justice for the woman. It didn't do much for her life, though. In spite of being released, she leads a lonely isolated existence, ostracised by family and the community.

The women who work at the centres and campaign against male violence are well aware of how these kinds of highly publicised episodes can be manipulated to become the 'Asian problem' and create a pathogenic view of black family life. The media tediously persists in equating domestic violence with arranged marriages – the modern-day equivalent of cannibalism – which helps to entrench further racist ideo-logies and relationships. The women from Southall Black Sisters argue that the systematic violence and humiliation which denies women autonomy and perpetuates conditions in which women are kept dependent on men for their sur-vival are the same for all women, regardless of their com-munity, culture, race, class and religion (after all, white women's refuges started long before there were centres established for black women). However, what is different is the way religion, culture and traditions prevent Asian women from seeking help and independence by acting as constraining factors.

The role of the state in maintaining the vulnerable posi-tion of women is also considerable. The very term 'domestic violence', weightless and almost cosy in its overtones, indicates how the crime has been trivialised by society. Even when convictions are obtained, the sentencing is hopelessly inappropriate, and this perpetuates the victimisation of individual women. A woman in Oxford who was viciously attacked by her husband with an axe now lives in complete terror because he has been released after a couple of years.

As far as black Asian women are concerned, their plight is made worse by the racist attitudes and institutional barriers they have to face when they do decide to take action. According to the Southall Monitoring Group, for example, an Asian woman is more likely to be asked about her immigration status and whether she had an arranged marriage before she is asked to describe her problem. The racist immigration laws have also increased the dependence of some women on their husbands. Should they separate from their husbands they risk deportation if they haven't themselves been naturalised. It is an extremely potent threat that husbands can use against wives. Even in the so-called caring agencies there is pressure put on Asian women to conform to cultural stereotypes, even by those social workers and other professionals who describe themselves as anti-racist and who claim to have an understanding of Asian cultures. Their way of providing appropriate service to women from 'ethnic minorities' is often to interfere as little as possible and to 'respect' their culture. They pander to the dictates of the most reactionary elements in the community and this in fact means one law for whites and one law for black people. By using Asian 'experts' these agencies often put women back into dangerous situations because their culture demands it. They would not dare to treat white women in the same way, as conciliatory pawns in the name of peace. There is also well-tabulated inter-agency co-operation, for example, between the immigration and the DHSS, which works to deny basic rights to Asian women, who are often vulnerable because of language difficulties, a lack of awareness of their entitlements, and a general view that Asian women are easily pushed around. The Mental Health Act is also increasingly being used by husbands and obliging professionals, gullible and only too ready to buy their definition of deviant behaviour to control errant wives.

In many ways Asian women have initiated domestic changes and led the way for action against male violence. They have established the political rights of black women to organise themselves and deal with issues in the way they think will be most effective. They have not been afraid of direct action as a response to male violence; they have helped to bring the whole subject out from behind discreet net curtains and put the item on the political agenda, and most importantly they have helped to debunk forever the notion of the Asian woman as totally passive and in need of constant resuscitation by caring white people.

Sita's is a very personal and individual account. Her experiences are not explicitly linked to wider political analysis of why violence to women is accepted and why it is sheltered by the Asian community. It is not linked to the other struggles faced by Black people in this country, nor does it concern itself with the combative strength and resistance movements of Asian women to the state and community. It is our responsibility to lay down the context for such private accounts so that some light can be thrown on the multi-faceted nature of the struggle faced by black Asian women.

Also of interest

FINDING A VOICE
Asian Women in Britain

Amrit Wilson

'The book comes alive . . . for the first time Asian women speak for themselves, about themselves' – *Shaila, Wires*

'A must for seekers of a true understanding of the position of Asian women, for all feminists and, of course, for all Asian women' – *Perminder Dhillon, Morning Star*

This remarkable book tells of the past, of present adaptation, of old and new attitudes to love and marriage, of drastic changes imposed on family relationships and friendships for Asian women in Britain. Overlying and intruding into their daily lives are experiences of racism in housing and education, on the streets and at the hands of the law, in immigration policy and at work. In describing these attitudes and struggles, *Finding A Voice* also tells of the increasing militancy and organisation of these new members of the British working class. Amrit Wilson received the Martin Luther King Memorial Prize in 1978 for this moving and important work.